# A Light
# in the Mind

## *Living Your Life*
## *Just as It Is*

## Carolyn Atkinson

Everyday Dharma Zen Center
Santa Cruz, California

Published by Everyday Dharma Zen Center, 113 New Street, Santa Cruz, CA 95060.
www.everydaydharma.org

Cover and text design by Cliff Warner.
Cover calligraphy by Kobun Chino Otogawa Roshi.
Author's photo by Marcia Quackenbush.

ISBN 978-0-692-00758-7
Library of Congress Cataloging in Publication Data on file.
Printed in the United States of America

10 9 8 7 6 5 4 3 2 1

For All Those Practicing in the Tradition
of Kobun Chino Otogawa Roshi

# Contents

# Introduction
# A Basic Perspective

Recently, I had the most wonderful good fortune: my first grandchild was born. Now, of course, children are born all the time; it's an absolutely ordinary, everyday event. And, also, every time a birth occurs, it's truly a miracle. It's so amazing to be what we call "embodied." This word expresses not only what we are—we inhabit our animal bodies—but also what happens for us: we discover ourselves through being in our bodies. And this experience of being alive, of being embodied, is both exquisitely wonderful and, also, at times, profoundly painful. It's complex. It's exciting. It's frustrating and confusing, and it's also fabulous, to discover that we are anchored in this human form. We can see that we have birth and we have death—and our being embodied is that which lies between these two fundamental events.

I've been thinking about what it is to experience this living between birth and death as embodied beings. And I began to wonder what I could say to my wonderful new grandson that might be helpful as he, too, experiences this embodied life. I asked myself: what do I wish my Grandma had told me? What would have been useful? Is there anything essential, absolutely basic, to consider as we enter into these bodies and these lives?

It occurred to me that one of the most foundational teachings of the Buddha—called **The Three Marks of Existence**—is exactly what I would like to share with him, because, as much as I can understand these concepts, as frequently as I can remember them, and as often as I can internalize them, they help me with living my life. Sometimes we may hear grand-and-glorious, abstract explanations of these Buddhist teachings, but I'm thinking of an everyday teaching, something that even a child can understand.

So, what is this basic perspective? What can we usefully say about being in a body? What are the core "Facts of Life" the Buddha taught, in the most fundamental terms? I would put it this way: **there is one thing to *know* in our life; there is one thing to *learn*; and there is one thing to *do*.**

What is the one thing to *know*? It's very simple. Sometimes we're hungry. Sometimes we're tired. Sometimes we need help to stay dry and warm. Life can feel painful. Often we want things to be different than they are. Sometimes we need to cry—to get help, to express what we feel, or simply to soothe ourselves.

At other times, life is perfect. We're fed and rested and warm. We feel energetic and happy and interested in life. Someone who loves us is holding us. We hear the familiar voice of someone who cares for us. The world is a friendly, welcoming place. Sometimes life is this way, too.

So here is the one thing to *know*: life can be wonderful, and life can also be painful. Being in these bodies that are born and grow and age and die—being embodied—includes *all* these different feelings. And it's not right or wrong to have these experiences—to have an *embodied* experience—it just *is*. We're not making a mistake when life feels difficult. It's not our fault. It's not about our deserving to feel pain. And it's helpful not to believe that when things are going well it's because we're so special we made it happen! It's useful not to take blame *or* credit. Life is what it is. To be in a body—to be embodied—is both pain and pleasure. It is sorrow and joy. It is loss and gain. This is the first fundamental fact of life. This is how it is. This is what we can *know*.

What is the second vital fact? What is the one thing to *learn* that may help us in living our lives? It is that whatever we're experiencing—a wet diaper, a hungry stomach, tiredness, fear, or the satisfaction of a big burp, a full tummy, a hand rubbing our back, a soothing sound in our ears—whatever it is, life keeps changing all the time. When life feels unbearable, something shifts; and when it all seems perfect, something shifts also. When we notice our experience, this is what we see: everything born into a body has the nature to change. As long as we are embodied, nothing will last forever—not pain, not pleasure, not sorrow, not joy, not ignorance, not wisdom. And when we say to ourselves, "I want only waking up, I don't want sleep," or "I want only warmth, not cold," it's like saying, "I want only the in-breath, and not the out-breath." When we try to hold on to one part only, life can be very painful. So this is the thing to *learn*: everything keeps changing, as long as we are in these bodies.

The third core teaching from the Buddha is usually explained in this way: "We are all interconnected," or, "We are not solid, separate selves." But a friend of mine has a slightly different explanation that I like very much: "Don't take it personally." This is the thing we can *do*. Let's don't take *life* personally. Let's not automatically assume that if we feel hurt or afraid or lonely or frightened, it's because we are bad people. If someone strikes out at us, it doesn't have to be about whom we imagine ourselves to be. Let's not take all the painful knocks of life personally. And I would suggest that, if we are flaming successes, it's good not to take that personally either. We don't have to blame ourselves, and we don't have to praise ourselves. Life is not our fault. And it's also not our credit. It is what it is. It's good not to believe that life is something we can or even should control. Life just happens—to all of us. When we do this, when we don't take it so personally, life can be much more peaceful. It can be both more satisfying and less frustrating. If we don't take it personally, this embodied life, we will find we come much closer to being happy.

So here is the basic perspective: *one thing to know*—life is made up of all our experiences, both good and bad, and it simply is what it is; *one thing to learn*—it will all keep changing; *and one thing to do*—don't take everything so very personally or get too upset about life. This is really very clear and not abstract. A child can understand it. We all can understand it.

And, yet, I find it can be easy to lose sight of this fundamental view. I sometimes long for things to be different than they are. I feel myself pull away from life now and then. Do you experience this too? I have to keep making a conscious effort to remember. I have to keep practicing all the time. I suspect that this, too, is what it means to be human, to be embodied in this world. We have to continue practicing our whole lives. We try. And, then, we try again. And it helps me to share this undertaking with others. We speak of this often at Everyday Dharma Zen Center—the power, for each of us, in practicing together. So, please join me here in exploring what it means to be embodied in this life, and to remember again what the Buddha taught: one basic thing we can know, one basic thing we can learn, and one basic thing we can do.

# 1
# The Winds of Impermanence

Each summer, for a number of years, I've approached late July with a mixture of feelings: sadness, longing, appreciation, wistfulness, and an increasing sense of acceptance. This is the time of year when my Zen Buddhist teacher, Kobun Chino Otogawa Roshi, died unexpectedly. On July 26, 2002, Kobun was visiting at the home of a student when his young daughter fell in a small pool in the backyard and he jumped in to save her. His heavy robes pulled him down, and both Kobun and his daughter drowned. Each year, the anniversary is a reminder to me about how fleeting life is, how impermanent everything is.

Kobun's death was a complete surprise. The news traveled quickly among his long-time students, and we discovered how shocked we were that life could be this way. I remember exactly where I was when I heard the news; I remember my disbelief. Kobun had been a rock-solid part of my security, so I found myself thinking, "How could he die?" How could such a thing happen? It was unbelievable, and, emotionally, totally unacceptable!

And yet…and yet, it was true. He had died. Birth happens, almost always a wonderful event. But death occurs too. Endings arrive. Birth and death and everything in between—all of it together makes up our life experience. The death of someone close to us, someone beloved, someone on whom we rely—this especially can remind us how transient life is. We notice how the winds of impermanence blow through our lives, over and over. When death comes, we are confronted with this basic truth in a way we cannot deny.

And clear though this fact of impermanence is, it is nonetheless difficult to remember. I find that my mind wants to believe that what I rely upon is permanent, that it will always be there for me. It may be something as simple as the Saturday Farmer's Market—"How could they ever stop having the Market?" I may ask. Or it may be a most beloved teacher. My mind longs for permanence. But in those moments when I can remember how impermanent it all is, how quickly everything can change, I find that I also remember to be more grateful, to wake up again. Thinking of Kobun and his unexpected death reminds me to wake up again.

A few weeks ago, I had an opportunity to feel this experience of impermanence. My husband, Alan, and I went on vacation to one of our favorite places in the Sierras. I love being up high in the mountains, with all the craggy rock formations, the cool breezes, the particular plants that grow there. There's manzanita, a ground cover that looks like a stumpy cousin of our coastal Madrone trees with its waxy leaves and red bark. And there are the tall, weather-gnarled pines, the great sky, the high-altitude meadows and the deep cold lakes. I love all of it.

But there's one place that's my special favorite, in the Plumas National Forest. I try to go there as often as possible. It's quiet and relatively unpopulated, with wonderful hiking trails. This year, there happened to be forest fires nearby and a large fire burning at a lower elevation, near a town called Paradise, made the air quality especially poor for several days. There seemed to me something symbolic about a fire in Paradise, but I couldn't decide what the symbolism might be! In any case, the air cleared as the week progressed, and we were able to begin hiking after a few days.

Walking the familiar trails, I was amazed to see how many wildflowers there seemed to be this year. We passed a local couple on the trail coming down the mountain, and they told us excitedly that the wildflowers were the most beautiful and profuse that they could remember—a combination of early rains and other factors had produced an unbelievable beauty. The woman said it hadn't been this wonderful for the past fifty years. And, apparently, the flowers were the most exquisite in my favorite area, near Long Lake just below Mount Elwell. So we immediately turned ourselves in that direction, to visit the wildflower fields.

It was truly a paradise when we reached the meadows, away from houses and fires. The flowers were magnificent! We saw whole fields of wild baby blue delphiniums swaying in the breeze. Queen Anne's lace covered entire mountainsides. Near the water sources, there were hundreds of tiny red and yellow columbines, and miniature orange tiger lilies curled in on themselves. Whole, huge swaths of color swayed in the winds. Entire fields of flowers, perfect flowers, were everywhere. I was so grateful to see all this, to have the opportunity to be in this exact spot, knowing how rarely all the conditions come together to form this exquisite beauty. And thinking of Kobun—the unexpectedness of his loss—I was acutely aware that we never know if we'll get to see something beautiful again. I asked myself, "Will I come back here once more, at just the right time? Will I be able to hike up to see them again? Will the flowers be the same?"

Kobun's death and the physical beauty in the mountains, as they came together in my awareness, created an explosion, in which I felt the great impermanence of it all. Fifty years to create this particular richness of flowers, and, then, actually being here and seeing them, at just the right time. Sixty-five years of living for Kobun, and then his life was over in a moment. I felt acutely aware of how fragile and impermanent life is. And I found myself wanting to remember it all. I wanted to look so closely, to see so deeply, to remember so well, that I might…what? Well, that I might keep it all, forever. I don't carry a camera any more when I hike, but Alan had his cell phone, so I asked him to take pictures of the flowers. There it was—that wish for permanence again, the desire to hold on to that one perfect moment. We do this, don't we? I'm talking about that wistful feeling that can arise when we notice the sheer beauty of life, the wish to never forget, that longing to keep these perfect moments forever.

A little further along on the hike, we came to a big waterfall area. Several groups of people were there, and one couple in particular was moving from place to place, posing in front of the different waterfalls. First one of the couple, then the other would take turns standing in front of the background. They were walking through the landscape with an eye to setting up pictures and capturing the moments on their camera. I completely understood. I felt it, too. We want to hold on. Alan offered to take their picture together, and they were grateful. Perhaps we'll hold on to perfection a bit longer, if we take a picture of it.

It's a common human wish never to lose beauty, to hold on to joy, to cling to peace, harmony and love, and to the people we treasure. If we could just stay in that one perfect moment, we say to ourselves, then…. It's a very human longing. Basho, the famous Zen poet who lived in the seventeenth century, wrote about this basic urge when he said, "Even in Kyoto/ Hearing the cuckoo's cry/ I long for Kyoto."[1] We do long to hold on. When Kobun died, I couldn't believe it. I'd wanted to keep him forever. I'd assumed he would always be there for me. And, yet, we discover that it's impossible to hold on to anything—*everything* is eventually swept away by the winds of impermanence. The photographs never quite seem to capture the feeling of the day itself. People we love and treasure disappear. Flowers bloom, then fade and fall apart. Summer passes inexorably into winter. Perfect vacations inevitably come to an end.

This is just the way it is. When we really pay attention in our lives, we can notice what Gerard Manley Hopkins was pointing to when he wrote, "There lives the dearest freshness deep down things."[2]  And we cannot hold on to this dear freshness, to what we love, to any of it. It all comes, and it all goes. This might seem rather depressing, seeing clearly that we can't hold on to anything. But, actually, what I experience when I look directly at this constantly changing nature of life, when I really recognize and feel this impermanence—both of pleasure and of pain—it has the effect of making life both more precious, and much less serious. We can't control life. We can't make things be the way we want them to be. All we can do is show up for what's happening. We can only pay attention to life, just as it is.

To continue the story, when we returned from the mountains, from the perfect beauty of the flowers, I got to experience another kind of impermanence—something I would have much preferred to avoid! I turned on my rather elderly computer to do some writing, and my old iMac decided it was the perfect moment to commit suicide. Each time I clicked on an icon to go to a particular file, I could see the system melt down right before my eyes. When I dragged the mouse to an area on the screen and touched it, it was as if the files turned to water and began running uncontrollably, disappearing into a void. I reached toward the screen, and said out loud, "Stop! Wait! Where are you going?" I tried to hold on. I wanted to keep having my computer work, as much as I wanted to grasp the beauty of the wildflowers. Now, I'm not a computer jockey. I know what I need to know to do my writing, but beyond that, it's a mystery to me. So when the files melted and disappeared, everything in my day and in my week had to change. I couldn't write the way I usually did, and I feared that all my files would be lost. I've been assured this isn't true, but it could be. Sometime or other, it could be true. We learn, over and over in these summer days, that fire can take away what we love in a moment. A simple pool of water can snuff out the life of someone precious to us. We can lose all our hard work in a quick moment of computer-generated death.

This is the way it is. We cannot hold on to anything in this changing life. On the most mundane level, I couldn't stop my computer from melting down before my eyes. And I couldn't stay in the Elysian flower fields forever, either. We cannot cling to any one moment, whether we are in a place of beauty or a place of sorrow. We cannot prevent this life from changing. What we *can* do, is pay attention to our minds. We can learn to notice our experiences in the midst of our lives. We can observe, and we can feel the longing, the clinging and the pushing away right as it's happening.

Why does this matter? Well, I find that when I really notice this basic insight the Buddha taught—that everything keeps changing—when I feel it in my bones, in my gut, or wherever it is we feel these deep truths in ways that make them more than just intellectual ideas, I discover that I begin to love my life much more than I might otherwise. And it seems to me that this happens in two ways.

The first way is this: yes, the flowers—the baby tiger lilies, the swaying columbines, the blue delphiniums—are so beautiful in the moment we are with them, and then they are gone from our sight. But we don't have to miss the experience of seeing them. In the beauty of the flower fields, I noticed my impulse to take pictures—an impulse that sometimes takes the place of simply being present itself. I felt that clutching, the longing to hold on. And, then, I knew in that exact moment that I was seeing this enormous beauty I couldn't hold on to, and I felt deeply how wonderful the experience was. By noticing these precious moments while they're happening, in all their joy and sometimes in all their pain, I don't seem to feel regret later on. I don't have to wish that I hadn't missed this one unique life in front of me, while I was living it. All of us can notice, right in the moment as it is happening, the great trembling beauty of being alive, the way the tiger lilies wave in the wind on the mountainside. And, by noticing, we don't have to regret missing our life.

The second way is that when things change, and I've been able to be present in my life, I no longer feel the change is quite so much my fault. When we notice that the winds of impermanence blow constantly, that sometimes difficult and painful things happen, as well as wonderful and beautiful things, when we feel our longing to hold on, or to get away to avoid the pain—when we notice all this, we also discover that we are not inadequate or bad people. We're not failures. We are just human. We are just like all the other people taking pictures, and all the other people clinging to their computers. We're just like Basho in Kyoto, longing for Kyoto.

So we don't have to take everything quite so personally, or so very seriously. We can't control anything, really. Not our computers. Not the wildflowers. Not the fires. Not the pools of water. These human minds, this is what they do. They long. They cling. They pull away. *We* long. We cling. We pull away. This is what all of us who are members of the human family do. We're not especially better than others. And we're not especially worse. We're just ordinary. This life we live is quite ordinary. And, also, it is quite precious. We are quite precious. And this is a relief. It's a big relief. It's good to be just one more ordinary, precious member of the human family. Even in Kyoto, hearing the cuckoo's cry, we can long for Kyoto. Even among the wildflowers in the Sierras, we can long for the Sierras. Even here, in this very life, we can long for our lives, while the winds of impermanence continue to blow.

# 2
# Inhabiting
# Our Lives

A few days ago, I went downstairs to my office, turned on my computer and sat down in my chair, when suddenly a dreadful chainsaw whine began right outside my window. It was very loud, close, and quite unpleasant—a high-pitched screech like fingernails on a chalkboard. I listened for a while, then the sound stopped. "Well, maybe," I thought, "it's just a quick event." I set up a new file, typed the date at the top, but as I began to write my first sentence, the noise started again. I walked to the window, and discovered a man working right next door to me, pruning a very large Monterey pine. They're beautiful trees that grow fast, and, within a few years, develop a thick trunk and big branches. I thought, "OK, some pruning is needed. That tree's overgrown its space, and it's for my neighbors and I like them. I'll do a few other things and it'll quiet down before too long." So I did some chores around the house, but, unfortunately for my literary efforts, the whine of the chainsaw kept going. So then I thought, "All right, I'll just go run the errands that I was planning to do after sitting at the zendo."

I went to the grocery store and the drug store. I went to our zen center and sat for noon meditation. I was gone quite awhile and I was pretty sure the noise would be over by the time I got back. But it was still going on, and I saw that what I had thought was a quick pruning job was actually an entire tree removal. It was still really loud in my office, and it was definitely far from being finished.

Eventually, of course, it did end, after several hours. But I noticed something interesting as I reflected on this small experience—maybe you'll recognize what I mean about this common, mundane, daily kind of event. As I was listening to the noise of the chainsaw, I realized that I was adjusting my life and planning what I would do, "Just until things get better." I was waiting until the world around me seemed more opportune for what I had planned. I was waiting for life to be a little bit different than it actually was.

There are two aspects to this experience of adjusting to contingencies. One is the willingness to adapt to changing situations, and to live our lives in relation to the world as it is. We have to learn to do this, because things keep happening all the time. It's a skill to adjust, to be flexible and responsive. It's rather like the movement in Aikido when someone's coming toward us, in which we learn how to step aside to allow the other person's movement to carry him or her forward. We let the energy flow through. Something changes outside, and we respond, and this is a very helpful attitude. Life is a bit smoother when we don't get bent out of shape easily, or struggle and fight against everything that comes our way. And a lot comes our way. It's skillful to be flexible.

But there's another aspect to this coping behavior. Sometimes we're waiting for things to get just a little bit better than they are. We're waiting for life to somehow change here or there, to be more exactly the way we would like, and, *then*, we say, we will be able to live our lives. Then we will undertake the Great American Novel. Then we will begin exercising. Then we will be happy. Then we will *really* live.

I had lunch recently with a friend of mine who is past traditional retirement age. He's actually seventy-five, and has been doing the same art-craft work for more than forty years. It's a difficult field to be in, constantly relying on promoting your craft work to make a living. He has to convince others that they need what he makes. He also teaches in one of the local schools and has done this for years too. Yet he says that, even with all the time he's spent at his school, he's never felt really welcomed by his colleagues. He doesn't feel seen by his students or by the public, and he has never experienced that his work is appreciated. This is what he said to me at lunch: "It all feels like dust in my mouth. All around me people get recognition for what they do, but it just doesn't happen for me. I think maybe I need to start over. I need to reinvent myself. I've been thinking about moving somewhere else, where people will appreciate what I do more than they do here. I feel like my whole life has been a failure. I just haven't found my way."

Now, what I know from the outside is that he *is* respected. He's not famous, but he's not completely unrecognized. His work definitely is valued on a local and perhaps on a regional level. Still, it's not enough for him. It's not quite right. It's not the particular kind of recognition that he craves. And his life, he says, is "dust in his mouth." He feels like a failure. He's waiting for that one *other* thing that has always eluded him. If he could just get *this* particular kind of professional recognition, then he could feel like his life is worthwhile, and, then, he could start living his life. But he's going to be seventy-six soon and he may not have a whole lot of life still to live.

My friend's story may sound stark and extreme, but, I would ask you, are you also waiting for life to be just a little bit different? To get one particular thing done that's bothering you, that you'd rather be finished with? Are you waiting for the chainsaw to stop, and then you'll know what to write?

Often, when we really look at our minds, we're waiting for that "one other thing" that will make everything all right, yet that "one other thing" is a continually changing, evolving desire. We're waiting until we're finally able to buy a house. But then we find ourselves waiting until we pay off the mortgage. We're waiting until we have children. But then, fairly quickly, we're waiting for them to grow up. Maybe we're waiting to feel less angry. Or perhaps we're waiting to feel less depressed. Sometimes we're waiting for the next paycheck so we can buy that one item we really want. We might be waiting for the next drink so that we can feel relaxed, or perhaps we're waiting to stop drinking. Here's a big one: some of us are waiting until we lose weight. I know a number of people who are waiting to start their lives until they've dropped twenty pounds. I had one client in my acupuncture practice who was waiting to gain weight—that's more unusual. When he put on some more muscle, then he would start looking for a girlfriend. We could be waiting to be healthy. Or waiting for the right job, the right partner, the right situation. We're waiting for the pain to stop. Maybe we're even waiting to die so that we can be born again! Just that one thing and then, we think, and then—we'll magically feel different. We'll be able to finally be truly alive. We think, "Then I'll be happy! Then I'll be present in my life. When just this one thing changes, I'll be able to start living the life I want."

You know, I think our story is that then we will live happily ever after. It's a fairytale mindset, and I definitely have a big piece of that. I recognize it. There was a slow dance song when I was growing up that captured this romantic ideal. Those of you who are old enough will remember what a slow dance was—that great excuse for touching someone you had a crush on. The words went like this: "Suddenly, I'll know when my love comes along. I'll know then and there." It's from the musical *Guys and Dolls* and I loved that song. I really believed it. I would just wait and see, and, at some point, my life would feel just right, and, magically, things would be perfect. As the song said, I would *know*. It's touching, perhaps, to believe this when we're fifteen. When we're fifty or seventy-five and still waiting, perhaps it's even more poignant.

I heard Angeles Arrien, a wonderful teacher, say one time that we can easily use "spell words" to enchant ourselves in life. We say, for example, "If only.... " If only this had been different in the past, or if only I had made another choice. Or maybe we say, "When only...." When only something changes in the future, when only the chainsaw finishes, when only he stops doing this, or she figures out what her problem is. Using these phrases regularly, we can begin to be enchanted by our own words, as if we are in a fairy tale under a spell, waiting, just waiting. It's really possible to spend our entire lives redoing the past, planning the future and fixing the present. It's easy, in fact, to live under the spells of "when only" this one thing happens, or "if only" my life had been different than it is.

In my experience, it's breathtakingly difficult to be willing to be present here in this very moment, with just the ragged "is-ness" of life. Just *this* moment. Just *this* life. It's much easier to wait for something else, when we imagine we will *know* that things are finally right. I've been doing a practice recently of remembering and reminding myself, over and over, every time I can, that nothing different than this life is ever going to happen. There is absolutely nothing to wait for. This is it. I saw a cartoon recently of two monks sitting next to one another in meditation. One monk is obviously answering the unspoken question from the other: "Nothing happens next." We could say nothing is different from just this moment—while this moment is happening.

It's so easy to be waiting, always waiting, for life to begin, waiting for a slightly different life, or waiting for a change of mind. Maybe we're waiting to understand it all. Perhaps we're waiting for transcendent meaning to arrive. Or we may be waiting for a permanently quiet mind. Maybe we're waiting for enlightenment, and, if we experience enlightenment, then we can begin to wait for it to happen once again. Sometimes we're waiting to be loved completely, in just the right way. And, often, we're just waiting to be forgiven, to be accepted.

When I recognize this, when I can notice the *feeling* of my mind waiting, I begin to experience that it's the waiting itself that stands between me and my life. It's as if there's a tiny transparent membrane between me and the world, as if my mind is covered with plastic wrap. There's a small and flexible barrier between the experience of me and the experience of just being here. A great deal of the time we can be directing our attention to the past moment or to the next moment. Did you think of anything in the future while you meditated today? Did you think about something that happened recently? We can be very committed to fixing things just slightly, to searching for the next best thing that will make us happy, to seeking the next best understanding, so that we'll be safe from suffering, or from embarrassment, or from pain. Then, it seems, then we will be more than willing to live happily ever after.

So, think about this for a moment: *this is it.* Right now, right here, just this. This is our life. When we step out of this room, and we put on our shoes at the door, putting on each shoe—that's it. That's all there is. There is nothing else waiting to be better than putting on our shoes. There's nothing else. This is our only life. Are we sleepy? Are we discouraged? Do we want something to be slightly different? I can promise you, it will never be different in exactly the right way. If I wait for the chainsaw to stop, then maybe my energy won't be just right for writing. Or maybe the room will be cold. Or the phone will ring and I will have to take care of something. Everything keeps changing, and life is almost always not quite perfect, not just yet.

If we really want to inhabit our lives, if we are really willing to be in our lives, these very lives, we have to undertake a massively courageous act. We have to be willing to let this life be enough, just as it is. I encourage you to undertake this practice. There isn't ever going to be a "happily ever after." I'm sorry to bring you this news, but we will *not* get life exactly right; we will *not* fix everything so that it all comes together beautifully. So, if you catch yourself waiting for life to be different than it is, remember this: there is nothing to wait for. There is nothing else better than this life right now, painful as it may sometimes be, because, right now, nothing else exists. Nothing happens next. Once in awhile, life can feel as if we're getting a tooth filled without novacaine! Is this still it? Yes, it still is. It takes enormous courage to stay present, to keep choosing to be in this very life—in this one, the only one we've got.

Here's what I'm suggesting: we put on our shoes. We get the filling put in. We feel the sun on our skin. For a moment, we breathe, and we feel at ease. And then sometimes, yes, pain arises. And then, at other times, we feel incredible joy. Then, in the very next moment, the fog settles over the land. And then we die. And this is it. There is no other life to be waiting for. Feel it for just a moment—there is nothing else but this. So don't wait for things to be better than they are. Don't wait for things to be different than they are. This fabulous, terrible, possible, present moment— this is exactly our life. This is it, the only one we've got. Think of this the next time you put on your shoes. Or the next time the chainsaw starts up. Remember, this is it. Nothing happens next.

# 3

# Are We
# Safe Yet?

I have a good friend, a colleague from my former acupuncture days, who is a skilled practitioner here in town. He's well known and widely loved, and his professional life has been largely very rewarding. But he recently and unexpectedly had a difficult, tangled encounter with a long-term client. The client became increasingly unhappy with him, and finally denounced him to some of his colleagues, which was incredibly painful for him. So, a few weeks ago, he and I met for lunch to discuss what was happening. He went carefully through the entire story, reaching back to the beginning of his relationship with the client. As we talked, he was able to see how his deep, unconscious childhood stories had led him to believe that he could "save" this client from the core pain she was experiencing. He also saw how her particular ways of asking for help had fit into his old belief systems; it was a natural response for him to try to rescue her. And it was probably inevitable that it would all lead to discomfort and disillusionment in the end.

As we talked, my friend began to see what his choices were now, in this painful situation. None of them are choices he would like to make, but at least it's clear that he has a few options, and he outlined the next steps he will probably take. As he stood to leave, he said, "OK, I get what's going on. I see the roots of my old story, and the ways I'm getting tangled up, and I see how I can deal with what's happening. I don't like it, but I can do it. But I just want to know that I'm never going to get caught in this situation again!" Don't we all wish that? I know I do. Something painful happens and, yes, OK, I can deal with it, but at least I'd like a guarantee that I won't have to feel this exact pain ever again. I want to be certain that I'll be safe.

The difficulty is, there is no guarantee that we won't get caught again. Life is a continuing experience of new events, and each time these events look just a tiny bit different. Nothing ever happens in exactly the same way. It well may be that the same thread is catching us, but each time it has a new and distinct appearance. It's amazingly easy for our habit energy to take over, so that we become caught in our old patterns, again and again. Still, I know I would like to have some certainty, some safety in my life. Couldn't I just not make the same mistakes over and over? Couldn't I at least learn from my mistakes?

Security and safety are fairly universal longings, I suspect. I hear many people expressing a wish for something they can always count on when things get difficult. It's a natural impulse. One area in which we can see this desire for safety and certainty, at least in our Western culture, is to look at the booming insurance industry. Do you have insurance of some kind? I have health insurance, auto insurance and homeowner's insurance. And I'm glad to have them. If we think about insurance, it's really about protecting us from the unexpected, from loss, from suffering—often from financial suffering—but from suffering of some kind. And, of course, being alive, we don't know what's going to happen in the future. Lawsuits can come our way at the drop of a hat—in one single moment of inattention. It may be as simple as turning our head one way instead of another in a car at a certain moment. Or a major illness can bankrupt us. Or our house might burn down, and, without insurance, we might never be able to afford another one. So, yes, we carry insurance, and it gives us more security, a greater sense of certainty that, at least financially, we can get some help when catastrophes strike. Prudence makes sense; planning for the unknown is reasonable.

However, it's also possible for prudence to become paranoia. The selling of insurance has gone to some extreme lengths recently, and I want to share a few of these "options"—isn't that what they're called?—with you. I ran across several articles about some creative new forms of insurance. I'd like to be very clear that I am not making these up.[3]

An article in the BBC News in April, 2002, stated that one insurance firm "offers cover against supernatural (and alien) activity."[4] The article explains that the policy covers death, injury and damage to personal possessions from extraterrestrials. Another form of insurance is available which offers up to 1 million pounds if the policy holder can prove that he or she has been transformed into a vampire or werewolf. I think that taking out such a policy suggests an amazing presence of mind, both to be able to anticipate such an event, and then to hunt down an insurance policy for it!

There's also a pub landlord in England who purchased insurance to protect his staff or customers in case anyone is killed or suffers permanent disability "caused by ghosts, poltergeists or other abnormal phenomena on the premises."[5] The pub is allegedly haunted by the ghost of a monk who hanged himself in one of the rooms. The policy is provided by a company named "Ultraviolet," which has actually paid such claims in the past, including one for an incident in which a woman died in her home, and it was concluded that a ghost was responsible for the crime.

Finally, it's also possible to purchase John Wayne Bobbit insurance.[6] Most of us remember what his problem was, and it occurs to me that if you're in a relationship and you're buying this insurance, your relationship is probably in trouble. Things might not be working out so well. However, different strokes for different folks—

literally—in this case. Aren't these all incredibly creative attempts to be safe? What wonderful illustrations of our very human quest for certainty!

It's likely that the desire for safety is universal. It's not just humans, of course; we know that animals learn to stop suddenly so they won't call attention to themselves, and many have amazing protective coloration. They learn how to run or fight or hide. We all want to be safe, don't we? And many of us humans want to know what's coming in the future. But here's the thing: we *don't* know and we *can't* know what's coming next, because, by definition, *it hasn't happened yet!* Here's what Helen Keller thought about security. "Security," she said, "is mostly a superstition. It does not exist in nature, nor do the children of man as a whole experience it."[7] This is a helpful explanation: security is mostly a superstition. But it is a superstition to which I certainly cling, to which I think many of us cling, as we hope, as my friend was hoping, that we won't have to experience again whatever has been painful in our lives.

So, if we can't rely upon insurance to save us, and if Helen Keller is right that we can't rely upon having a safe and known world, then the question is, what *can* we rely upon? I could say that you can rely upon meditation. Or I could say that you can rely upon Buddhism. But, at some point, the likelihood is that you will feel this too has let you down. Sometimes I hear people say that meditation doesn't "work." In a very difficult situation, it can feel like nothing "works." We can't always keep things clear within ourselves. This doesn't mean that meditation is useless or inadequate, but life keeps changing. It's always new, and we're living in these limited bodies and these habitually conditioned minds, and we don't know what's coming next. Sometimes we're tired. Sometimes we can't pay attention anymore. We can't always get everything right, and we can't avoid change in our lives. And, interestingly, this is what the Buddha taught, right up front. The First Noble Truth is about *dukkha*, the Sanskrit word that is translated as "dissatisfaction" or "discomfort," even sometimes as "suffering." This is life, the Buddha taught. Life is like this— inherent in life is *dukkha*—the experience that nothing works all the time. This is the way life is.

We could ask, then, is there *anything* upon which we *can* rely? Is there certainty anywhere? Is there something we can trust? Is there any place of refuge in this life? I remember hearing a teacher at a retreat say this simple phrase: we can absolutely trust that life will be whatever it is. We can take refuge in life exactly the way it is. We can at least count on this, and I find this makes great sense.

But what does it mean? When I think about taking refuge in life as it is, and letting life itself be my certainty and my corner of safety, I notice that this thought feels fine, it feels attractive even, when life is fine. It makes a lot of sense to me. And I notice that it's pretty good when life is pretty good, and it's OK when life is OK. But when something unpleasant or uncomfortable comes along, my first impulse is to fix it. And my second impulse, which follows within a moment or two, is to think that there must be some mistake. There must be something wrong if life is happening this way. Surely there is something I can do to make it better. Now, "something I can do" may be very subtle. It may occur to me that I'll fix it all if I just meditate more, or if I understand it better, or if I can calm my mind, or maybe if I can see things in a larger context. In other words, fixing things may mean working with what's happening so that it transforms in my mind, but, still, fixing it is my subtle goal.

But here's a more radical thought: we don't actually have to "do" anything, even something wonderful like reaching enlightenment. And we don't have to have a strong enough faith in a supreme being or in ourselves or in meditation. We don't even have to purchase the right kind of insurance. When we are willing to be in the present moment and aware of it, we can see that life is what it is, and *that's* what we can count on.

It's a strange kind of safety. It's an odd sort of security. In fact, when I can reach that point for a moment, it's a breathtaking kind of shift in my mind, to be—just here. And I really experience it as a powerful entry point into freedom. When I can be present and can notice what's happening, what I find is that, more of the time, I stop trying to make things be different than they are. And when I stop trying to fix things and change things and judge things, or when I stop trying to "understand" my way to something different, what I often discover is that my heart and mind can settle down into what's actually happening, right now. Amazingly, out of that settling down, I think some kind of healing can occur. And almost always it is not what I thought it would be. Most of the time, healing is not what I expected.

Now, this is difficult. I want to be very clear. I'm not suggesting that life is always bland and neutral and that if only we're equanimous, everything will be fine. That hasn't been my experience; that hasn't been my life. But I do find that when I can bring awareness to as many moments as possible, when I can bring myself to be with my life exactly as it is, or, perhaps more accurately, exactly *as it feels*, then I'm more able to be present with my mind in the very next moment, when it grasps or rejects the next feeling that arises. When I don't notice my experience of what life is, of what I feel, my mind goes almost instantaneously to the next step—to clinging and to resistance. And this is the place where suffering begins—in the wanting, in the rejecting. It's not that life in itself is so much of a problem. It's that I can move seamlessly and unconsciously into fixing and clinging, into trying to ensure that life will be only what I want it to be. It's so easy to jump into trying to be certain and secure.

So here's an alternative: we can trust life to be what it is. The difficulty is that we can't fake trusting life. We can't make it our next subtle project. When I really pay attention I can feel, over and over, my mind pulling back ever so slightly from my life just as it is. And I notice that, like my friend, I want assurance that the pain will go away and not return. I have to keep reminding myself that this is it. Here. Now. Nothing else. And it's OK, this needing to make the effort to remember all this—it's how we learn to be aware. I notice that when I can let this moment be just what it is, when I can let myself take refuge in life being the way it is, my shoulders relax a bit, my mind relaxes, my heart softens. I can choose more willingly to be in my life.

We practice resting in things as they are, and not leaping unconsciously over life as it is, into life as we want it to be. Mostly, I find that life is different from what I expect. Oddly enough, it often seems more bearable. Sometimes it's disorienting. Sometimes it's incredibly spacious. It feels like taking a deep breath without doing anything else—just breathing. And here's what I find: this whole process is not that easy to do, and, also, it's not so hard to do. But it's definitely different from what we normally do. So it's really about being willing to be in our lives, to stand up again in the middle of our experience. It's about standing up again in life, just as it is.

# 4

# Whose Cookies Are These?

A middle-aged woman was sitting in an airport waiting area one day. Her flight had been delayed a number of times, and she was impatient to get on the plane, but there she was, marking time as we often have to do, before she could finally board her flight. To get through the waiting period, she'd bought a book to read, and she had a package of chocolate chip cookies on the seat next to her—you know how we put things next to us on those long rows of seats? She'd dropped her purse there with the cookies, had her book in her hand, and had draped her coat over the seat back.

Now, a young man was sitting in the next seat over—this empty seat was between them—and he had put some of his things on the middle seat also, a newspaper and a small backpack. The waiting area was beginning to fill up, so they were forced to share the space. The woman looked curiously at him; he was engrossed in reading some technical magazine. She reached out and took a cookie, bit into it and it tasted quite delicious. She thought, "Well, this is a good way to pass the time." However, in the next moment, the young man sitting to her left took one of the cookies too, and munched away as he read his magazine. She felt startled and surprised that he was eating her cookie. She took a breath and waited, but he just kept reading, so she took another cookie and turned back to her book. But, then, he took another cookie too. Well, she began to get a little upset, which is understandable, right? She looked over at him with an irritated daggery look, the one that says, "What are you doing? I see what's going on here," but he didn't pay any attention. He just kept eating and reading. So she took another cookie, and he did too. She couldn't believe this was happening! Here was this stranger just sitting there, eating her food. And she found she was starting to rant in her mind, "Boy, this country has really gone to the dogs. We used to have some sense of propriety and decency. I remember that politeness was a value when I grew up, but people are so brazen now." We can really build up a head of steam when we feel righteous, and this woman found that she was becoming more and more angry.

The two of them continued to sit there, and after about half an hour, they came to the last cookie—one last cookie—and the young man preemptively picked it up, broke it in half, and handed half to her. She was stunned that he could do that, amazed that he was so pushy, and, then, to top it all off, he just ate the other half, without saying a word. She thought to herself, "Well!"—as my aunt used to say in Nebraska—"I never…!" I'm not sure what the rest of that expression is, but it's definitely one of righteous outrage.

*Whose Cookies Are These?*

The woman gathered up her things, stood up, glared one last time at the young man and stomped off. "I mean," she thought to herself, "casual is one thing, but piggish is something else." She paced around, feeling extremely irritated. Finally they called her flight and she got in line to board. When she looked around, she noticed that this young man was also standing in line a few spaces behind her. Although he hadn't looked at her when he was sitting next to her, when she turned and stared directly at him, he looked right back. And he actually had the gall to smile at her. She whipped around to the front, and waited while the line inched forward. When she came up to the ticket agent and needed her boarding pass she reached into her bag. She felt something there, but wasn't sure what it was. After she'd put her boarding pass into the machine and walked to the other side, she looked in her bag, and there was her package of cookies—unopened. Oops! She suddenly realized that she had been eating *his* cookies!

I really love this story because I can imagine it happening so easily. Often, we think we know how things are. We're quite certain we know what everyone else intends, and we feel very clear about what they said, what they did and what they will do. We know it all. So it's startling in those wake-up moments to realize that this "knowing how things are" actually prevented us from really being in our lives. This woman was convinced she knew what was happening. What she knew, unfortunately, just didn't happen to be true!

It's sometimes incredibly difficult to be with life the way it is. Maybe it's a matter of being embarrassed: they weren't our cookies after all. But sometimes being with life the way it is—not the way we want it to be or believed it was or must be—can be enormously painful. Someone said to me once, "I can't accept my mother's death." But here's the thing: her mother had died. So, what's the alternative to accepting what happened? As far as I can see, the only other alternative is to reject it. We can say, on a feeling level, "I refuse to accept this. I refuse to let life be this way." But rejecting isn't going to change unpleasant facts. The only choice we really have is to either accept or reject the way life is.

Part of the difficulty could be that we might feel as if accepting what's painful means we condone an action, are glad that something happened, or are saying that the behavior that led to this outcome is just fine with us. It's almost as if acceptance equals approval in our minds. So we say, "I cannot accept it." If our mother dies and we love her very much, it can feel almost like a betrayal to accept what has happened. But acceptance doesn't mean approval of an event; it's simply a recognition of what has happened. Think about the urgency that some of us feel about our planetary crisis. Many of us feel very strongly that we *have* to make every effort, we have to change, everyone has to change. But here's a chilling thought: it's possible that we will not, as the people on this planet, make enough of an effort. This, too, is a possibility. So, we can ask ourselves, "Then what?" And what I mean is, "Then what, in our minds?" If we reject this possibility, suddenly a huge part of life on this earth is cast out as being unacceptable. All the people who do not think the way we do are unacceptable. Life as it is becomes unacceptable. It's only all right if things go our way. I want to say this very clearly: the willingness to look directly at the possibility that we may not make it as a species, on the earth as we know it, does not mean we condone this outcome. It does not mean that we approve. It simply means that we are willing not to close down to life and to people and to the earth itself, whatever happens.

Sometimes it may seem that if only we wish hard enough or believe strongly enough, or just try even more intensely than we have, then something bad won't happen. If something's so painful that it seems inconceivable, and if we don't give a single bit of energy to considering it, then there's a better chance that this won't be the outcome. The problem is that this so easily becomes magical thinking, the "Norman Vincent Peale American Mind" or "The Power of Positive Thinking," as it was called back in the fifties. A few decades ago, this belief resurfaced as the New Age mentality. It's a recurring story in our culture, that we can manifest whatever it is that we think about.

Now, certainly I believe it's true that how we live in our minds generates much of what we experience in our lives. If we spend all our time hating people, our lives will be filled with hatred. If we spend as much time as we can practicing love and compassion, we will certainly, I think, feel more loving and more compassionate. The way we train our minds absolutely affects what we experience. But it's also true that life is what it is, not what we want it to be. Wishing hard enough is what we learned from Jiminy Cricket, isn't it? *When you wish upon a star…* I loved that song as a child, but life is much more complicated than this Fantasyland jingle.

We could ask, how do we know whether we're being realistic or optimistic or pessimistic or blind? I once saw a cartoon, a sketchy pencil drawing, in which a couple is sitting on a couch, and a woman is standing next to them with a tray and cups of tea. The woman on the couch is pointing to her husband and saying, "Donald is such a pessimist. He's convinced he's going to grow old and die." Now maybe Donald is a pessimist. Or maybe he's a realist. Or maybe he's an optimist. Maybe, actually, those labels aren't very helpful.

One factor that's useful to consider as we contemplate this question of acceptance or rejection is to notice the feelings around our response. Are we desperate to have things be our way? Is there a clutching, a clinging in how we react? If so, we may be entering that area where we're trying to force life to be what we want, rather than accepting what it is. We can believe that if we just try hard enough we will all live happily ever after, but, I have to tell you, that is not my experience, even though it's frequently been my wish.

In my medical practice over twenty years, I worked with and watched several young children die of leukemia. The question that came up over and over was, why do bad things happen to innocent people? What did these young children do to "deserve" such a painful death? Why, we ask, why did this have to happen? I frequently hear people say, "I can't accept that these terrible things happen." But this is my experience: every time we cannot accept what happens, every time we are certain that we know the way things must be, we put up a filter between ourselves and this ragged, changing, uncertain world. We cut ourselves off from it. We are no longer a part of the life that's all around us.

Certainly we can feel so much pain that it seems we can't bear it, but what are our choices? Our only other choice is to reject life as it actually is. Acceptance or rejection—these are our choices. Remember, acceptance does not mean condoning. Here's a statement from Rabbi Joseph Gelberman, who lost his entire family—wife, child and parents—to the Nazi Holocaust. He said, "Most of my colleagues brought Hitler with them when they came here to this country. They were constantly expressing anger and hostility, and eventually it killed them. But I wanted to make sure when I came to this country that [Hitler]could not kill me also. It wasn't easy, of course. We are trained to be angry when we experience loss or pain, and letting go of the anger took me years and years of thinking and praying. But this helped me, and perhaps it will help others. Moses gave his farewell address to the Israelites saying, 'I have spoken to you about curse and blessing, about life and death. I say to you, choose life.' So," said Rabbi Joseph Gelberman, "I chose life."[8] He chose, actually, to be present in and for his life. He chose not to close off to what happened and to what his life was.

This is what I keep discovering: life is more complex, more mysterious, more unknown than I ever dreamt it could be. It's so much larger than we can know through our personal filters. Our practice is cultivating the willingness to live in the light of not knowing, the willingness to choose this life—the one we have, not the one we want. I think much of the time, maybe most of the time for me, I just don't know what's happening, much less why. And life is whatever it is. Life keeps changing, and I don't know what will come next. I usually don't know what's happening now, and I realize how little I know what actually occurred in the past. I think I know how it is, what's been happening, and then I reach in my bag and suddenly—there are my cookies! All along I've been eating *his* cookies! We can be so certain about the way things are. Or the way things have been. Or the way things must be. But if we truly wish to reduce our suffering—and, I would say, also the suffering of everyone we come into contact with—we need to find, to uncover, to cultivate the willingness to be ruthlessly present with this raw, unfiltered life, just as it is. Not just when it feels good and wonderful, but also when our mother dies, when we feel embarrassed, when we feel ashamed about something we've done—and when we want so much for things to be different than they are.

Here's the thing: we still have a choice. Our choice is not about whether life is what it is, or whether life will be only what we want it to be. Our choice is, do we want to accept or reject what this life is? Most of the time, when we look at our lives we really don't know what's coming, and often we don't know what's happening or what has already happened. So, what is it like to live in the light of not knowing? What is it like to stand up in the middle of this very life, the only one we've got? Sometimes, it's painful. Sometimes, it's exhilarating. Sometimes, it's amazing. Often, it's funny. Sometimes, it's sad. Occasionally, it's breathtaking. Whenever I go there mindfully with my awareness, whenever I'm able to be there for just a little bit of time, it often truly takes my breath away. We so much do not know what the heck is going on most of the time. Did you eat my cookies or am I eating yours? I just don't know. Most of the time, I just don't know.

# 5
# Life Isn't Personal

In college, I was fortunate to be able to go abroad for my junior year to Vienna, Austria. I had grown up in an isolated town in western Nebraska; we had only one small bookstore, a couple of movie theaters and definitely no art galleries. So I spent much of that college year haunting the museums and galleries, making up for what I hadn't been able to learn earlier. It was fascinating to see the development of art over the centuries, and what became clear to me was how important the individual is to our Western way of thinking. Any quick tour through a Western historical art gallery can show us this.

For many hundreds of years, Western artwork focused on Christ and the Mother of Christ. There are numerous Madonnas throughout the ages—portrayals of Mary holding her beloved child. As we come closer to our modern age, we begin to move to other topics—kings and emperors and nobles and, gradually, we even begin to see portraits of commoners—but whoever the subject, the individual is at the center of the work. Think of one of the most famous paintings ever, the *Mona Lisa*. She wears an enigmatic smile and sits all alone. Or consider Michelangelo's *David*—that wonderful sculpture, larger than life and all by himself. He's very symbolic, in a sense, of the way our culture thinks. When we look at these Western works of art, we see that we keep circling around and around the value of the individual.

I used to hear people in my medical practice say, "I don't ever want to be dependent on anyone." Have you heard that too? As we grow older in this culture, it's common to dread being *dependent*. I've heard it often. Maybe we've all thought it at one point or another. We prize being independent. We value being autonomous. We aspire to be "self-actualized." Have you heard this phrase? Think of the glory in these words: "independent," "self-actualized." We are trained culturally to value these qualities. Most of us—not all of us, but many of us—live our modern lives in splendid (or less than splendid) isolation, meaning we don't live in family compounds for the most part. Frequently, we move away from our family of origin. We do our own work; we raise our own children; we hold it together sometimes in the context of a one-on-one relationship or, perhaps, all by ourselves.

Well-known developmental psychologist Margaret Mahler suggests that the goal of normal and healthy child development is separation and individuation—these very important Western cultural values.[9] Children grow up to have their own identities and make choices independent of others' influence. This seems healthy to us. We strive for emotional separateness. Sometimes this is called "differentiation." Therapist David Schnarch writes that, "Differentiation is our ability to hold our sense of identity while in close relationships with others."[10] We could say that to be distinct is to be outstanding. It's an important facet of our cultural value system. Recently, I came across an editorial in *The New York Times* by William Safire where he expressed this succinctly. He wrote, "He stands tallest who stands alone."[11] It's a very good description of our values. John Wayne literally acted out what we learn. He was, for many Americans, a kind of iconic hero.

What I'm describing is simply our culture. Here's another way to look at it: when we are emotionally ill in the West, it's often seen as having trouble differentiating ourselves. Do you remember that period of time in the late eighties and early nineties when we all were considering whether or not we were "codependent?" And being codependent was considered a very big problem. Many of us read the book called *Codependent No More*.[12] Now, my conclusion at this current point in my life is that I'm absolutely dependent on everybody! But being codependent became an issue in our culture during that time.

Or sometimes we say, "I am the child of this or that type of person," and we name the problems of our parents. Often what we're talking about is feeling as if we haven't been successful in individuating or differentiating or separating ourselves. We haven't been able to get away from our parents' views of the world, and, therefore, it seems that we suffer in our lives. Please don't misunderstand: these are completely valid issues for us to consider in looking at our lives. My point is simply that the stance of individuation and differentiation is a particularly important value for us.

Quite often, we measure our accomplishment of individuation in two ways. One question we ask is, Are we able to construct a strong sense of self? Most of us have looked at this question, at one time or another. Are we constructing a sense of self that is functional and coping, perhaps even heroic? And the other question is, Are we successful in making our lives "work out" in the ways we want them to? Those of us who prowl through bookstores have seen the self-help shelves filled with more and more books. And we have an increasingly popular societal niche being filled right now by people who are "life coaches." We get help from people who teach us—through books or coaching or in other ways—how to be strong and how to get what we want out of life. Here's something interesting: frequently, we turn to professionals for help when we struggle with knowing who we are, or with not achieving our goals. But we don't usually consider it a problem to be a high achiever. Have you noticed that? Those people are generally applauded.

I recently purchased a book called *Mean Genes* by Terry Burnham and Jay Phelan.[13] The authors tell a story about a man named Jim Clark: "Consider Jim Clark, who became one of the richest men in the world by starting Silicon Graphics, Netscape, and several other companies. Before he was bitten by the business bug, Clark was a Stanford professor earning low pay and dreaming of striking it rich. He told his friends that if somehow he could make a hundred million dollars, he would be eternally satisfied. When he passed that lofty goal, he reset his sights on a billion. Now, with billions in his pocket, he is working just as hard as ever and hopes to seize the title of World's Richest Human from Bill Gates. Having founded three different companies, each worth more than a billion dollars, Clark still toils."[14]

Clark's is a story of great success in our culture. Yes, we do value money, and, yes, we do value splendid isolation. And this book, *Mean Genes,* is not only an amazing summary of our Western values, but, also, an enactment of them. The authors are two highly accomplished young men, examples themselves of what they are writing about and what we culturally are seeking. In their book, they concentrate on achievement and coping skills by looking at genetic makeup. Genetic definitions seem to be our latest form of diagnosis—the perspective of this decade. In the nineties, we were obsessed with viruses; in the eighties, a lot of attention was given to the lowly yeast (*Candida Albicans*) in our systems. Before that we had hypoglycemia. It seems to me that what we look at, what we pay attention to, at any given point, tends to be how we diagnose. This makes sense, doesn't it? Whatever we look for, that's what we tend to see. You've heard the expression, "When all we've got is a hammer, everything looks like a nail"? Right now, with the enormous discoveries being made in unraveling the genetic code, we are indeed fascinated by genetics.

Let me share a few sentences from *Mean Genes* in which Burnham and Phelan lay out their thesis: "We call our own shots. Along with passions, genes have created willpower and the ability to control behavior consciously. With these uniquely human abilities, we can rise above our animal instincts. *Mean Genes* is a guide to doing just that. Step 1 is to understand our animal nature, particularly those desires that get us into trouble and can lead to unhappiness. Step 2 is to harness this knowledge so that we can tame all our primal instincts."[15] They conclude their book in this way: "We should enjoy our animal passions and even indulge them, but prevent them from controlling us. The key to a satisfying life is finding a middle ground that combines free-flowing pleasure, iron willpower, and the crafty manipulation of ourselves and our situations."[16]

When I consider this suggestion for the "key to a satisfying life," I am struck by how American this perspective is. And perhaps how youthful it is too. From the perspective of my life now, in my sixth decade, if I were shelving this book in my local bookstore, I might elect to place it in a section about humor or even fantasy! This is how likely it seems to me that I will find "free-flowing pleasure, iron will-power and the crafty manipulation of [myself and my situations.]" But the book is usually shelved under the categories of self-help, science or psychology. This is who we are—this is America.

We could conclude that I'm talking about a treatise on cultural values, so what does it have to do with you, and what does it have to do with me, and why is it important anyway? I heard a story about the Dalai Lama speaking with a group of Western Buddhist teachers who were asking him how to deal with the self-loathing so common among their students. The Dalai Lama apparently got a quizzical look on his face and turned to his translator, asking, "What is this? What is self-loathing? What does it mean?" Do any of us not know what it means? We all know what self-dislike is about. Imagine not knowing what it is to turn on yourself in anger or in judgment. This was what the Dalai Lama was expressing. Imagine a mind in which we don't condemn ourselves.

Here's what I'm suggesting: if we believe that we can create ourselves as separate and independent individuals, if we believe that we can be successful in making life be what we want it to be, then, when life is just what it is, not necessarily what we desire, we can easily turn toward self-loathing and self-rejection. We can experience a great sense of insufficiency, of isolation and of failure. You know, in our culture we have more tools and faster computers, more wealth than ever before, clean water and mostly enough food, a huge amount of mobility, enormous homes, and still… still, we are not happy. There are so many things—objects—we are striving to have. If we just look at our television ads, we see all the possessions, the trappings, as well as the accomplishments that would seem to make us successful and popular and happy. We learn, culturally, to believe that we need all these things in order to actually *be* happy.

The thought goes like this: if we are in charge of our lives, then, by definition, we should be able to get it right. If difficulties happen and we are in charge, then we must—we *must*—take it all very personally, because everything that happens is our fault. If we have the power to make something right, and instead it goes wrong, then it must be our responsibility. When I put it this way you might say, "Well, maybe this doesn't make sense." But, actually, I think this comes close to describing our basic cultural assumptions.

Now, here's something very important: when I describe this as our cultural pattern, I'm not saying this is bad. And I'm not saying that it's good. I'm saying that it simply *is*. This is our culture. I have to tell you that I am incredibly grateful for the opportunity I've had to individuate, to differentiate myself, because otherwise I might still be living in a tiny old house on a farm in rural Nebraska. I know I wouldn't choose to do that now. It's a very difficult life. Every once in awhile, I hear someone talking about how glamorous it would be to go "back to the land," and, you know, my experience is that it's tough going back to the land. It's not romantic. It's hard work, and it's exhausting. So, let me be very clear: I appreciate the opportunities I've had to "create" my life for myself.

And, yet, there's another side to this as well. I remember the deep pain and suffering I had as a young woman because I believed that I *had to* create myself completely from the beginning. I didn't know who I was. I didn't accept whatever I thought I was. So how could I possibly create this self, all by myself? It was enormously confusing and painful. And both of these observations go together. This is our life here in the United States.

Let's turn this over for a moment, culturally, and go to a more traditional place. What we well might find in a more traditional world is the enormous strength and comfort of an extended and linked social and cultural system. We might find a kind of safety. We might experience strong support. We would always know who we were and, often, in more traditional cultures, we would know that our family would be there for us, whatever happens. At the same time, it can be a highly constricting experience. As is sometimes said in traditional cultures, "The nail that sticks up gets hammered down." It can be painful and very confining. So, please hear me clearly. I'm not saying "bad" and I'm not saying "good" about either cultural pattern. I'm saying "is." Our culture *is* this way. This is what we have.

So, whatever our cultural perspective, there are consequences in terms of what we experience, what we notice, what we value, and where we struggle. When we believe something, that's what we tend to see. What we experience is very much governed by our expectations. Interestingly, we learn that the Buddha taught his disciples to pay close attention to their own experiences. Yet even this—our own experience—is culturally influenced.

I recently read a book I like very much, *Buddhist Practice on Western Ground* by Harvey Aronson.[17] He tells a story that perfectly illustrates this point—that we experience what we notice, and that what we notice is part of our cultural training. He writes: "Several years ago I participated in a week-long Chinese Chan retreat— which is Zen in China—attended by both white Americans and ethnic Chinese. At the end of the retreat, the master asked each participant to express what benefit he or she had derived from the retreat. The white Americans spoke uniformly of how the long hours of meditation helped them get in touch with themselves, gave them strength and sanity to cope with the pressures of society, and assisted them in the process of self-realization. The Chinese contributions were very different. The first Chinese woman broke down in tears as she spoke. The week of meditation had made her realize how selfish she usually was. She wanted right then and there to bow down and apologize before her family. She wanted to perform some act of deep repentance. The statements from the other Chinese people similarly revolved around feelings of shame and repentance. When the master asked the Americans if they felt shame and repentance, one person replied with a touch of impatience in his voice, 'You always ask me that and I always say no.'"[18]

Isn't that interesting? What we actually experience is not necessarily "objective" at all, but is strongly influenced by our culture. There's a metaphor I like about the mind being similar to an auditorium, and our awareness, what we are conscious of, is the area highlighted by a single spotlight roaming over the darkened theater. The spotlight moves around, and what we notice, what we see, is what the light shines upon. But this doesn't mean there's nothing else in the auditorium. There's a lot happening that we're not seeing. What we notice is what the light illuminates. Each of us notices what we learn to see, and what we learn to see is governed in good part by our cultural upbringing.

I want to briefly share what I hear from you about what you see, what you feel, what you experience. First, it seems that, in general, we all want our lives to work out, and we feel as if we should be able to make this happen. We long to get it all fixed—to be a good parent, to be a good partner, to not be a victim. We think that, if only we get a particular thing fixed, then…then it will all be good. As a consequence, we often feel responsible when life doesn't work out. We feel guilty; we feel disappointed; we feel depressed.

Second, we usually take our life experiences very personally. People say to me, "Why did this happen to me? Why can't I do better? What can I do to make it work out for me?" Sometimes someone will say, "Why am I always being punished?" or,

"I deserve to have bad things happen." Sometimes we think the opposite, "I deserve to have things go well. What's wrong with this picture?" All of these responses hinge on the belief that we are solid and real and should be able to make our lives be what we want them to be. If we don't get this or that to work out, then we are failing.

And, yet, when we look closely, we see that failure is built into these bodies. The nature of being born is that we will die. Old age, sickness and death come for all of us. In our culture, however, this is largely experienced as a problem. What do we say about the dying process in our culture? We say someone is "failing." That's the way it's spoken of in my family tradition. "Aunt Bertha is failing." It means she's dying. But we say, "She's failing." This is the way we interpret our lives. However, when we look closely, we see that we're simply part of the fabric of life. Our parents, our family, our origins, our gifts, our weaknesses, our hopes and dreams and expectations, and our cultural experiences—all of it affects us. All of it *is* us. And life is what it is. We cannot *make* things happen in a certain way, as much as we may long to do so.

At the end of the *Heart Sutra*, the mantra that closes the chant is this: *Gate, gate, paragate, parasamgate. Bodhi Svaha.* A standard translation is often: *Going beyond, going beyond, going all the way beyond, over to the other side. Wisdom. Hooray!* My teacher Kobun Chino Otogawa Roshi used to translate this mantra in a different way. He said: *Falling apart, falling apart. Everything is falling apart. Everything is always falling apart. Nothing to do.* We could say that life arises and it passes away; life comes together and then it falls apart—over and over and over. And Kobun said: *Nothing to do.* I've always taken such comfort in his translation. It gives me permission to live my life as it is, not as I imagine it ought to be.

But I think I would like to change just that last little ending. I would suggest that it matters enormously what we do, how we focus our minds, where we put our attention, and what we choose to do with our minds. There *is* something to do— these twin Buddhist practices of cultivating awareness and quieting the mind—and it matters enormously. Nevertheless, we can't *make* anything happen. It's all quite impersonal, this life. There's a line in the *Tao Te Ching* that I often think of that says: "Do your work, then stand back—the only path to peacefulness."[19] Let us do our best, make our very best effort, and also remember that it's not personal, this life. Then, let us stand back—this is truly a powerful path to peacefulness.

# 6

# Creating
# the Self

A few days ago, I went downtown to do some errands, after our noon meditation. It was a lovely Santa Cruz day. I walked to the local bookstore, and, as I was browsing along the aisles, a former acupuncture client came up to me. It was wonderful to see her. We exchanged news, and when I told her about the Zen Center her immediate reaction was, "I don't know how you do that meditation thing! I would absolutely go bonkers if I had to sit still that long. It sounds like torture to me!" We laughed together and parted after a few more minutes. Her reaction is fairly common—"How can you stand to sit still and be quiet for so long?"

Walking down the street a few minutes later, I ran into a rather shy computer friend of mine. We greeted each other and caught up on our news. When I described our Zen Center and the community to him, he responded, "I don't know how you can do all that community-involvement stuff. I would hate to have to see the same people and talk with them about my life. Ugh—no way!" We laughed together too, and each went on our way.

Here were two opposite reactions to the same description—one said she couldn't stand to be silent, and the other said he couldn't stand to talk. Both of them were quite emphatic about what would be uncomfortable to them, and they were at opposite ends of the spectrum in their experiences. I thought afterward about how this experience of discomfort with living happens for each of us, now and then, no matter what our perspective. We create our selves, we construct our selves, and then, having made this great effort, we frequently feel dissatisfaction in being the selves we've worked so hard to construct. We say, "I couldn't stand to do this," or, "I couldn't bear to do that." It's not that someone else is making us feel this way. It's we ourselves who feel uncomfortable, whatever these "selves" are.

This brings up an interesting issue—what is this "self," anyway? It can be confusing when we begin to examine a bit more closely this experience of being embodied. What exactly do we mean when we say, "myself"? How do we recognize ourselves? How do we, in fact, construct this self—this thing that we call "I"? We often say words of introduction such as, "I am Mark" or "I am Mary" or "I am Chris," and it can seem as if we know who we are. We're this living being walking around who's been given a name as an identifying tag: "Ken" or "Victoria" or "Fred." That seems to be fairly clear.

But we change our orientation slightly when we say, "I am tall," or, "I am female." This is more a recognition of ourselves based on an attribute; we're marking how we are recognized in relation to other people, often by physically recognizable qualities. We might say next, "I have blue eyes," and, all of a sudden, the self is an owner of the blue eyes—there is an "I" that owns a part of this self that "has" blue eyes. We may go on to say, "I am an architect," and all of a sudden this "I" that we recognize is identified by our actions, by our work, not simply by what we look like. If we say, "I am in love with so-and-so," our definition is based upon feeling. Or we may describe an event, saying, "I was beside myself with fear," and suddenly there's a split that's happened and we have two selves—one beside the other. And so on and on it goes. When we listen to our language about ourselves we can recognize how very confused we are about who we "really" are.

Now, part of the confusion is that the word "I" has different meanings. In one sense, we're talking about what we might call the psychological "I." This is the self that functions in the world, that makes decisions and carries them out. This "I" goes to work, prepares dinner, attends family reunions and votes in elections. We often arrive at our understanding of who this psychological "I" is by paying attention to our individual experiences, our backgrounds, our habits, our training—all the societal and social aspects that influence us in our interactions with the world. So let's call this the worldly functional "I," or the psychological "I."

The second self, the second "I," we might call the metaphysical "I." This is the self the Buddha was teaching about during his lifetime. Harvey Aronson writes: "Peter Harvey, in his meticulously researched *The Selfless Mind*, states that the picture emerging from the early Theravadin discourses shows the Buddha encouraging his disciples to explore their own experience and see if they can find a self, defined as '[A]n unconditioned, permanent, totally happy "I", which is self-aware, in total control of itself, a truly autonomous agent, with an inherent substantial essence, the true nature of the individual person.'"[20] This is the metaphysical "I" that we're talking about. The Buddha is asking, can you find a part of yourself that is real and solid and permanent, a self that is unchanging and will always be there?

In the early Buddhist discourses, what we hear is that his disciples looked and looked and then they replied, in effect, "No, Your Reverence, it is all transitory. We can not find a permanent self." What they were looking for, what the Buddha asked them to seek, was this second definition of self, this metaphysical "I." Their conclusion was that no such solid, permanent and unchanging self could be found. This is the Buddha's teaching that we translate into English very commonly as "no self." The Sanskrit word is *anatman*. And it means exactly this: the self is transitory. It is impermanent. It is not solid and fixed. This self is constantly changing; we can't hold on to it forever.

Why does this matter? The story we hear in the Buddhist tradition is that a young man, Siddhartha Gautama, searched and searched for understanding about his life, and then finally he sat down under a Bo tree and vowed that he would not stand up again until he understood the roots of human suffering. He was asking, "What is the fuel that fires human suffering? Why does it happen?" And the answer he came to was this: it is because we are attached to the belief in an enduring self, in a solid metaphysical self. We keep looking for something permanent, and we can never find it. This, he taught, generates our suffering.

I want to be really clear: the Buddha was not asserting that we are figments of our collective imagination. He wasn't suggesting that the disciples gathered around him did not exist, even as they shared their lives together. And he was not teaching that we should give up functioning in the world. He was saying instead, "Look at the place where we want the self to be permanent, where we want to always be this same, certain self, because exactly *here* is where we will find our place of suffering."

So, we're talking about two different kinds of selves, two different "I's." One is the functional, daily-life self, and the second we might name the essence self. In some traditions, this essence self is called "the soul." In some traditions, it's considered the "inner self." As far as I can tell, in studying and reading, and in listening to others and in living my life, this idea of an essence self seems to be a repeated, recurrent, consistent human longing. I suspect it's built into the very nature of our beings, as we become conscious. And here's the issue: when we read Buddhist teachings that say, "Give up your attachment to the self," or perhaps we hear, "The point of practice is to become selfless," or someone says, "You should give up your attachment to ego," these teachings are meant to be pointing to this metaphysical "I," to the concept of *anatman*.

But we can easily hear those directives as being about our daily functional selves. We may believe, for example, that this means we should give up interacting with the world. Sometimes people get involved with Buddhist practice and begin to believe they should give up all self-assertion, or learn to be totally passive and silent. Some people interpret it to mean we should almost give up being conscious. "If you're really enlightened you'll be, like, all zoned out and cool, dude, like, you know, Zen. Far out." This is a confusion that frequently happens.

And, sometimes with the best of intentions, Buddhist teachers get confused themselves. Certainly psychological problems around behavior can arise in long-term communities. And it's fairly easy for the holders of authority to insist that these functioning psychological issues are really metaphysical problems. It's not uncommon in Buddhist centers to hear someone say, "If you have a problem with such-and-such, then that's your practice." And this doesn't just happen in Buddhist communities. It can occur in many intentional communities. These issues can be very confusing. What is the functional self and what is the metaphysical self? It's difficult to be clear about this; we blur them together.

Another confusion for us as Westerners can be traced to Freud, who talked about the *id* and the *ego* and the *superego*. In modern American English usage, I think it's common to blur these words together. We use "I" and "self" and "ego" pretty much interchangeably. And it's easy for the word "I" to become "ego" and we know that "ego" can become "egotistical," and that "self" can become "selfish." It may seem that, subtly, and yet suddenly, the self is a negative experience for us. We can easily mix together in our minds these concepts about self and I and ego. And then we may confuse our psychological functioning with a metaphysical longing, and the results frequently lead us to feel badly about ourselves. We're not sure why we feel uncomfortable with ourselves, really, but we do. It all can become very painful.

Have I been sufficiently confusing here? If the answer is "yes," then I've succeeded, because I think this "self" is very confusing! In light of this complexity, we well might wonder how we are to understand ourselves in these lives. How can we make any sense out of this at all? I think that, minimally, we can say that, clearly, we are all in this life, together. All of us, every one of us, no matter where we live or what we do or what we believe, we are all born and we come to an emerging consciousness at some point. We become what we call "self-aware"—aware of our self as an entity in the world. I have a memory of this happening for me when I was eight or nine years old. We had hot summer nights in Nebraska, and there was no air conditioning then, so the windows were wide open. I remember lying on my bed, listening to the voices of the family next door—their house was just a few feet away—and I kept wondering why I was me and not Mary Sue Mohler, whose bedroom looked out upon mine. Why was I me? Why was I not her? I'm sure many of you recall those early self-aware thoughts, the times when you began to wonder, "Why am I me, and what is this life, and what is this being alive all about?" Then we grow up, and we keep trying to figure out how to live these lives, and who we are, and how we can make our selves—this "self"—be what we want to be, or perhaps be what we think we should be. We all get to do this, each of us, and it can be painful; it can be confusing.

If we grow up in a more traditional culture, the question may be directed in another way. Someone told me once that her issue of self was communally oriented: what should I do to be a worthy member of my family, so that I will never besmirch the family honor? This woman grew up in a traditional Asian community. In this Western culture, we often ask, "How can I distinguish myself? How can I be uniquely me so that I'm different from everyone else, so that everyone will recognize me?" But, wherever we live, wherever we grow up, we get to create a sense of self. Certainly, we must face the psychological and practical questions of how to live, of how to function in the world. And with consciousness also come the deeper questions: what is this thing of being alive, and who am I, and why am I me?

A number of you have shared stories with me about your ongoing experiences of creating this self, and of being this self. I want to share a few of these delightful tales. One of you described driving to a party recently and how, on the way there, in the car, you were rehearsing in your mind what you would say when you arrived. You suddenly realized that you were planning how to be yourself at the party. Figuring out how to be Chris, perhaps, or Catherine. Deciding how to be Monica. I thought that was a wonderful description. We do have such thoughts—I think one of the most common internal monologues is about what we will say and what we will do, in order to be ourselves.

Another person wrote to me about this question of self, "For the last few days, my mantra's been, 'It's all about me.' If I am judging myself for this, it's less than I ever have, and that feels good. I must say, I'm impressed. Even when I'm doing an act of kindness or sharing with others, the focus is almost always on myself. In conversation I wait, usually impatiently, for my turn to speak. When I'm with my partner or our children, I'm half there, with the other half thinking about me. When I'm working, I'd say I'm lost in self-analyzing about 75 percent of the time, and when I'm in my habitual behavior, huge amounts of time, hours and hours a day, are spent in morbid reflection on my particular life's trials. When I write, it's to sound good, much of the time, and the same with speaking. I'm self-obsessed. It's all about me." That's a great description, don't you think? Most of us could have written this. Yes, indeed, it's all about us.

Perhaps you've heard the story about a man at a party who is talking and talking about himself to a woman he's trying to impress. Finally he pauses for a moment, then says, "But enough about me! What do *you* think about me?" This is what we do, right?

Someone else mentioned to me that she was frequently silent in our meetings because she was concerned that, if she spoke up, she would blast everyone out of the room. She wasn't talking about coming on strongly or being critical of others. No, it was that she thought to herself, "They will never understand what I'm saying, and, then, what will people think about me when they find out how truly weird my mind is?" Have you ever thought that? We may hesitate to let people know what we think, because then they may discover how strange we really are!

Who among us hasn't worried about what others think, and who hasn't planned ways in which we will be ourselves in the future? Who hasn't felt self-obsessed? It's easy to want to be special. Don't we all want to be cared for and valued and appreciated? I tell a story in my book *Quiet Mind Open Heart* about my friend who took care of his mother in Nebraska. When we talked together and he cleared away all the caretaking and problem solving and could finally look directly at what he wanted, he said, "I just want to be good enough. I just want to be good enough for her."[21] We *do* want to be good enough. We want to be loved and appreciated and held in high regard. And we want these feelings to last forever. No wonder we suffer.

Here's one more tender story: recently, I went to hear Pico Iyer read at the Capitola Book Café. He was sharing his new book called *The Open Road*[22] about the Dalai Lama, and Iyer's wonderful to hear. I really enjoy what he writes. My favorite book of his is *Video Nights in Kathmandu.*[23] So there we were—many local Santa Cruz people—gathered together at the Book Café, and I invite you to imagine yourself a member of this crowd. It's a large group of people who've arrived, and they're very appreciative. As I look around, I see many people whom I recognize—old faces, familiar faces, what I would call "Buddhist faces"—people I've met in one way or another over the years. There's lots of gray hair in the crowd now, we're all aging a bit, it seems. There's an eagerness in the audience as we wait. Friendly nods pass around the room as people recognize each other. Hands reach out. Hugs are exchanged.

And now, here come the moderator and Pico Iyer up to the front. He's introduced, and begins to speak to us about his craft. He's a journalist. He's traveled to be here with us tonight. He talks about how important independent bookstores are for those like him who are writers trying to make a living. He speaks warmly about Capitola Book Café, and most of us nod our heads in appreciation. He's very engaging and entertaining, and he makes several personal comments about the Santa Cruz area, which we love. We feel a connection, a very strong connection, with him and with each other. He makes a quip about losing his hair, and we laugh. The

*A Light in the Mind*

audience laughs with him and he laughs with us. He tells us stories about the Dalai Lama, engaging and touching stories. We are moved as we listen. There are occasional sighs as he speaks, and frequent nods. We feel connected to him. And, when he answers questions, he does it so well, giving us lots of information and sharing his compassion and outlook on the world.

Finally, he finishes, and we all applaud and stand up to honor him. We're crowded together and we lean toward each other and begin talking. I turn around to greet a dear old friend who arrived a bit late—we couldn't connect beforehand. Some people move quickly into line to buy a book, and then to speak with him. Others turn to the door and step outside. I'm one of those. I move into the darkness, one of the early-departing ones. I turn around and look back from the darkness into the brightly lighted Book Café, and I see energy and talking and movement and lights and life. Then I turn again into the darkness. Here's the darkness, I think to myself. Each of us will be going home to our houses in the darkness, maybe going with someone else or maybe going home alone. And Pico Iyer too—perhaps he'll go to a hotel for the night, traveling from one venue to another. We just shared time together, all of us—an hour and twenty minutes of a very creative and appealing self-presentation by our author. He was charming and we loved him. We sat admiringly and looked at a "self" that we could all appreciate. People had listened intently to his words, heads had nodded around the room.

It's really so poignant, all of us gathering here, being ourselves, wanting to feel connected, to be seen, to be recognized, to be understood. Perhaps many of us tonight were rehearsing how to be our selves, how to do better, maybe how to be a little bit more like Pico Iyer. Then we turn and we go into the darkness. We go home, we go to bed; and the self that we have constellated, whether audience or author or all of us together, this self shimmers for awhile and then it gradually melts down a bit. I would imagine it even melts down for Pico Iyer. "There," he might think, "that went well tonight." And then he feels the out-breath. Then there's the exhalation, and the self stands still. And, then, the self drops down a bit, the self gradually dissolves again. You see what I mean? The self that we create over and over—no matter who we are—the self shines for a time, and, then, after the shimmering, there's this drifting down into silence.

My friend in Nebraska only wants to be good enough. We all really only want to be good enough, and "good enough," meaning loved and recognized, does happen for a time now and then. But good enough so much feels as if it needs to be solid and forever, and we can never quite get there—to that permanent, essential and unchanging "I." So this gathering together of self, this creation of self, rises up, and then it drifts back down. And this isn't bad. And this isn't good. This is simply the human condition. Within these bodies and these lives, we cannot hold ourselves together in a solid and permanent essence. It doesn't last. It cannot last.

Notice when you walk out of here tonight, into the darkness, into the silence, notice when you go home and lie down to sleep, notice the feeling of the self drifting down. I think of all of our stories, all of our efforts to be ourselves, and I feel such a huge tenderness for how difficult it is to be alive. Here we are, all of us humans. We try so hard. We create what we hope is good, and sometimes we feel the self shimmer up and we know—this time, this time it's really good. This time, we are loved. And, then, we eventually all go out into the darkness. We must exhale. And this self, this shining self we've created, drifts slowly back down. There is nothing we can hold on to. Nothing lasts. And this is the tenderness of member-ship in the human family. This is the way it is. Not bad. Not good. Just the way it is. We are all on this journey together.

# 7

# The Water
# of Our Lives

I recently came across a story told by David Foster Wallace, a contemporary writer.[24] It goes something like this: Two young fish were swimming along one day, chatting back and forth as fish do. They were just being adolescent males in a fish-like sort of way, scoping things out and looking to see if there were any young girl fishes nearby—you know, just hanging out. And, as they swam along, they happened to meet an older fish coming in the opposite direction. The older fish nodded at them, and, as he passed, he called out, "Morning, boys. How's the water today?" Well, the two young fish didn't say anything, because sometimes fish are this way too. They swam on for a bit longer, and eventually one of them did a flip in the direction of the other and said, "What the heck is water?"

The older fish called out, "Morning, boys. How's the water today?" and the two young fish were startled. "What the heck is water?" they asked.

David Foster Wallace told this story in a commencement address he gave at Kenyon College in 2005. He then reassured the audience of graduates that he was not the wise old fish. "The immediate point of the fish story is merely that the most obvious, ubiquitous important realities are often the ones that are hardest to see and talk about."[25] He's suggesting that sometimes that which is most fundamental is also the hardest to notice. "What is water?" the young fish asks. Well, it's obvious to us, we who are non-fish; we could describe water in quite a number of ways. But the question that arises for us is, what is it that *we* are not seeing? What are we overlooking? What are we so accustomed to, in our lives, that we don't even realize it's there? What are we missing?

This is a very good question: what is *our* water? I'd like to suggest that what is so fundamental for us—*our* water—is this: our experience of life is an interpretation that we make, based upon our own minds. We notice that life keeps changing and that it's always new, and, yet, often it can seem that life is very familiar. "Isn't this the way things always go?" we may ask ourselves. "Don't people always let me down?" "Don't I usually feel hurt?" "Doesn't he usually get angry?" "I'll never be good enough," we can think. Or, "If only I just get one more thing done or if only I buy one more thing, then…" and we swim on and on in the water of our own minds, of our own stories, of our own emotions and interpretations. Often we don't realize how much the experiences we have in our lives are being shaped by our very own minds.

Perhaps you've heard about the studies of lottery winners that show that even becoming a millionaire doesn't seem to affect long-term happiness for people very much? The same appears to be true with misfortune—after an initial adjustment period, most people return to their basic attitude toward life. Here's an interesting observation from a teacher in Singapore named Shi Qin: "In fact, everything we encounter in this world with our six senses is an inkblot test. You see what you are thinking and feeling, seldom what you are looking at."[26] In other words, when we look out at the world, what we see is much more a projection of our own minds, rather than any objective and external "reality." So, we could say that we swim in the water of our own minds—this is the medium in which we live. Life's not just about what happens externally; it's also about what we believe inside. And these beliefs that shape what we see are very much the fruit of what we cultivate in our minds.

The Buddha went straight to the point. Here's a version of what he said about this: "We are what we think. All that we are arises with our thoughts. With our thoughts we make the world. Speak or act with an impure mind"—or, we might say, with an unaware mind, or with an unconscious mind—"and trouble will follow you as the wheel follows the ox that draws the cart. We are what we think. All that we are arises with our thoughts. With our thoughts we make the world. Speak or act with a pure mind"—with an aware mind, or with an attempt to be conscious—"and happiness will follow you as your shadow, unshakeable. How can a troubled mind understand the way? Your worst enemy cannot harm you as much as your own thoughts, unguarded. But once mastered"—once noticed, or understood—"no one can help you as much, not even your father or your mother."[27] In our modern Western culture, we frequently look beyond our nuclear families for help, so we might say instead that no achievement can help us as much as our own minds, not fame, not wealth, not power, not fortune, not the right marriage or the right profession or the right connections. In other words, wherever we look for help, nothing can lead us more directly to happiness than understanding our own minds.

These are powerful words. We are what we think. We experience what we learn to notice. And we see projected onto the world that which we are actually thinking and feeling inside. The obvious conclusion, then, is that it matters a great deal how we train our minds. It matters whether or not we pay attention to what we are doing in our minds. It matters very much, because what we pay attention to is where we live. It is our water.

In Wallace's graduation speech, he goes on to say that "in the day-to-day trenches of adult life, there is actually no such thing as atheism. There is no such thing as not worshipping. Everybody worships. The only choice we get is *what* to worship."[28] And he explains that choosing a god or a spiritual path, or a set of ethical principles, is a way to worship that won't weaken or destroy us, because worshipping other things such as money, or possessions, or our own beauty or intellect encourages us to remain unconscious. With such a focus, we become more and more narrow in how we measure value, and less and less satisfied as time goes on.

What he's calling "worship" is another way of saying, "What we value, what we pay attention to, what we notice." And it's true. Value wealth above all and we will always be too poor. Value only power and we will always feel weak. Value nothing but sexuality and we will never be attractive enough. Value intellect alone and we will be vulnerable to seeing ourselves as inadequate. This is the way our minds work. This is the water we swim in, the way we measure experiences through a system of our own desires or longings or needs. If this is true—if we see what we learn to notice—then it's really helpful to begin to turn the mind toward the activity of noticing itself, toward awareness of what is happening in our lives.

How do we do this? I'd encourage you to notice each time you anticipate an outcome. Notice what you do when you feel this anticipation. What does it feel like, to want things to be the way *you* want them to be? And when do you find yourself rejecting things as they are? Notice your relationship to your mind and to your life. In other words, I'm asking you to observe the ebb and flow, the very water, if you will, of your mind in response to this ever-changing life.

What do you find to be the *nature* of your water, of your mind? Is it ongoing anxiety? Is it chronic fear? Is it anger just looking for a target? Is it wanting and craving and longing—in other words, desire—and never getting enough? Or is it pulling away, resistance, rejection? We often call this quality "aversion." These are animal instincts that operate for all of us, and, like water for the fish, we often don't even notice that these things are in our own minds. We jump right to the place of believing that it's what *they*—the other people in that world outside ourselves—are doing. It's what's happening *out there*, we think. This is the problem: we don't notice the very water in which we are swimming, in which we exist. We don't notice the impact of our own minds on our own lives.

I want to emphasize that swimming in the water of our own minds is a completely normal aspect of being these embodied human beings. We're not going to reach some place of unassailable objectivity, of permanent equanimity. We all have fears and wants and hopes and griefs. This is natural. This is human. However, it helps very much to be *aware* of what we are doing in our minds, of what our water is. "Oh, here it is—here's my water again!"

The Buddha taught that, "We are what we think." How we think is vitally important; and, to work with this, of course, we first need to know *that* we are thinking. This is the first basic awareness. We have to know that we're thinking and feeling. And, then, we need to notice *what* we are thinking and *what* we are feeling, and what stories we are telling ourselves about our lives. The awareness that comes with mindfulness and with the clear noticing that can arise with stilling the mind—*this* is how we come closer and closer to knowing our minds and our hearts, to quieting our minds, to opening our hearts, to seeing the water. "Oh…this is it. This is the water. This is the water in which I live."

Thich Nhat Hanh once wrote: "Our true home is in the present moment. To live in the present moment is a miracle. The miracle is not to walk on water. The miracle is to walk on the green Earth in the present moment."[29] And he concludes: "It is not a matter of faith, it is a matter of practice."[30] I really like this quotation. It suggests that we can bring our attention and awareness into the present moment, and exactly here—right in this body and here in this life—we may be able to notice the water of our lives. Our true home, this water, is not something other than what we have. We don't need a miracle to be present in our lives; we don't need fantastic experiences. And we don't have to take anyone else's teachings as the truth, or commit ourselves to blind faith. We can actually discover this water—our water, the water of our minds—through our practice, this training in simple attention and awareness. "Oh, this is my water. This is the water of my life." Learning to understand our minds and lives is not a matter of faith. As Thich Nhat Hanh says, rather, it is a matter of practice.

Atul Gawande, a talented surgeon and writer, published a book called *Complications: A Surgeon's Notes on an Imperfect Science.*[31] Here's part of what he wrote: "There have now been many studies of elite performers—international violinists, chess grand masters, professional ice skaters, mathematicians and so forth—and the biggest difference researchers find between them and lesser performers is the cumulative amount of deliberate practice they've had. Indeed, the most important talent may be the talent for practice itself. K. Anders Ericsson, a cognitive psychologist and expert on performance, notes that the most important way in which innate factors play a role may be in one's *willingness* to engage in sustained training. He's found, for example, that top performers dislike practicing just as much as others do…. But more than others, they have the will to keep at it anyway."[32]

This last sentence might well read: they have the *willingness* to keep at it anyway. In other words, the only difference may be in our *willingness* to practice. Every one of us can make this choice, and probably has made it, once or many times. In fact, each time we return to this practice, we are demonstrating our willingness to pay attention. It's not a matter of faith. It's not about special skills or grand illuminations, and it's not about extraordinary talent or vision or occult understandings. It's about the willingness to practice. We practice training our minds in attention and awareness, and we commit ourselves to the discipline of this practice. Attention, we could say, and awareness, and then the willingness to continue practicing—this is how we keep noticing. This is how we keep remembering: "Oh, here is water. This is water. This is my mind. This is my mind." We are what we think. How can a troubled and unconscious mind understand the way? Our own worst enemy cannot harm us as much as our own thoughts, if we are unconscious. But, as we work with our minds, as we practice remembering—"Oh, OK, this is water. This is water. This is my mind."—nothing else can help us as much.

David Foster Wallace concludes his commencement speech in this way: "None of this is about morality, or religion, or dogma, or big fancy questions of life after death. The capital-T Truth is about life *before* death.... It is about the real value of a real education, which has...everything to do with simple awareness—awareness of what is so real and essential, so hidden in plain sight all around us, that we have to keep reminding ourselves over and over: 'This is water.'"[33]

I want to encourage you to value this meditative practice of awareness and attention and the willingness to maintain your effort. I agree with Wallace that it is difficult to stay conscious and alive in the world each day. How do we stay awake and aware? We practice. We practice and practice. We try over and over again. This doesn't mean our lives will be without pain. And it doesn't mean that we will always like the outcomes we experience in our lives. But this is where we begin. "Oh, here it is. Water. This is water. This is my mind. This is my mind reacting. This is what I am doing with my mind and with my life."

As we practice, we come to know our minds better. We can see, "Ahhh look, here it is again. I pull away here, and I want this and I don't want that. I'm open here, and here I'm closed." This is where we begin, a little bit at a time, again and again and again. Very simply. And then there's this also: sometimes we find others with whom we can practice, and we can then undertake this effort together. We can simply train ourselves to notice: "This is water. This is the water of our minds. This is the water of our lives. You help me to notice it, and I'll help you."

So, please remember the Buddha's concluding words: when we bring our awareness to this noticing, then "nothing can help us more." This is very encouraging—nothing can help us more than awareness. Let us undertake this practice again and again, and let us undertake it together. I'm confident that nothing can help us more than simply recognizing, moment by moment: "Oh, this is it. This is water; this is my water. This is the water of my life."

# 8

# With Our Thoughts We Make the World

We've spoken about a very important teaching from the Buddha: "We are what we think. All that we are arises with our thoughts. With our thoughts we make the world." I'd like to raise the question now of how we actually understand these words. What do they mean? Someone recently made reference to this teaching by saying, "We create our own reality." This is a common way to paraphrase these words, and, often, this interpretation can feel liberating—it seems that we really are able to generate what we want and need in life. But this same idea, given a different context, can also be a source of great suffering. We must be very careful with the words we use, because both possibilities—liberation and suffering—can be enhanced by what we say to ourselves about our lives, by exactly how we understand this teaching.

I'd like to tell you a story that relates to this topic, and I would ask you to notice the thoughts that arise for you as you read it. This story happened to a friend I've known for a long time. It occurred a number of years ago in New England, but it's quite a timeless story, it seems to me. The elements are universal. I've known this man, David, since my early college days. He's a good and kind man who has lived a life of service to others. He's also a gifted artist and someone I admire greatly. David has a strong marriage, two grown children, and a profession as a successful printmaker in a lovely rural Connecticut village. He was very actively involved in raising his children; in fact, he did perhaps more than half of the parenting, since his wife had to commute to Hartford on a regular basis for her work. Because David was a printmaker and had his own shop, he was able to be an available parent, while still keeping his studio open and functioning. Of course, as is common with many artists, he's always done most of the work in his studio himself: stocking supplies, answering inquiries, shipping prints, everything needed to keep a small artisan practice surviving.

When David's children were teenagers they had a lot of friends. They were close together in age—just a year apart in school—and, with many friends in common, their family house became a kind of unofficial gathering place for the local kids. David was very supportive of the young people. He's not only a printmaker, but also an experienced writer who's always loved words. So he agreed, at his daughter's request, to help tutor one boy in learning how to write. This boy had not had a positive family experience at all. He had been in and out of various juvenile facilities as a young child. There were big gaps in his education, and he needed help to get ready for college. So David began the tutoring project in the spring of his daughter and her friends' senior year.

The summer following their graduation, David hired a group of these young people to paint his studio, which hadn't been painted in many years. None of the kids knew how, but they were eager and acquired the skills, and David funded them as they learned how to paint houses. By the end of the summer, they actually had a thriving business in the community. David was truly helpful to these young people. He was kind to them, and his children were proud of him. That fall his daughter went away to Smith College and David experienced something of the "empty nest" syndrome—he felt a bit disoriented after spending so many years being responsive to the children. With extra time on his hands, he discovered, as we might expect, that he could pour more of himself into his printmaking. He would often work through the day, meet his wife for dinner, and then go back for several more hours of solitary and pleasurable work in his studio.

Fairly late one night in October, David was still working when he heard an unusual sound in the back room. He started to turn around, but before he could even move someone attacked him. It was up close and personal—a brutal attack with a knife. He was stabbed several times. The attacker ran out, and David managed to get to the phone to call for help. The response was prompt and he was taken to the hospital for immediate care. After coming out of surgery, David was quiet for a long time. When he finally spoke to the officer in charge, he said that he thought he knew his attacker. Although the attacker had his head covered, David had recognized the movements, the eyes. He suspected it was the boy he had tutored in writing, who had also helped paint his studio and had been in his home many times. The police investigated. They were able to track the attacker down, and it turned out that he was indeed the young man that David had helped in many ways.

So, right now, notice what your thoughts are. Are you thinking, "Why? Why did this happen?" Are you thinking, "Well if only such-and-such…." Are you thinking, "No good deed goes unpunished." Are you thinking, "What did he do to cause this?" Just notice, if you would, what you are thinking about David's experience.

Here's the way the story continues. In the police investigation, several pieces of information eventually came to light. One was that this young man, who had just turned eighteen, had made several attacks on other people, but this history had been sealed by a court order, because he was a minor when these attacks had occurred. Hence, nobody knew about them. A psychologist who worked for the police department spent a good deal of time talking with this young man, and began to see that the attacks were all similar in origin and in pattern. It seemed that when life felt unbearable to this boy, he would attack the last person he remem-

*A Light in the Mind*

bered who had been kind to him, and David had been the last person to be truly kind to this boy before circumstances again caused him to lash out. It has taken David years to recover. Physically, he will never regain full use of his right arm, the one with which he does his basic printmaking, so he has been forced to give up his profession. His breathing will always be labored, because of damage to his lungs. David also reports that it's now very difficult to feel safe in his home. He is troubled at night, and repeatedly locks the doors. As you might expect, this was an experience a person doesn't forget easily!

Imagine if this were you. What would you learn from this experience? How would you understand it? The Buddha says, "With our thoughts we make the world." If we believe this means we "create our reality," and if this young man very deliberately chose David to attack, as we know he did, then did David create the circumstances of his attack? Was it somehow *his fault*?

The point I'm making is that it's easy to say we "create our own reality" when everything is going well. It's a way that we can feel really good about ourselves and about our lives. But what about when we get cancer? What about when a tidal wave destroys our home and kills our entire family? What about when we are attacked? Do we create our reality then? Did this good man, this kind man, create the attack that was so traumatic in his life? How do we understand this teaching from the Buddha?

Having had cancer three times myself, I've thought about these issues a lot. I've struggled with the questions of blame and responsibility, and I'd like to share some of my observations. The first thing I would say is that when difficult things happen, it's a natural, human tendency to ask, "Why do bad things happen to good people?" And it's understandable to want answers, so we can once again feel safe, so the universe makes sense, and so life is somehow orderly and can be relied upon. Religions are one of the places to which we often turn for answers to these big questions: "Why?" we ask, "Why is life like this?" In many traditions, the answer is, "It's God's will. We can't understand everything that happens, but it's God's will that this person should suffer." And, sometimes, although it might seem odd standing outside of it, this belief that someone suffers because God wants it to be this way can provide great comfort. It means that, even if I don't understand the particular circumstances, nevertheless, the universe still makes sense.

In Buddhism, the answer frequently given is "karma." This concept is often used to explain the unexplainable. Why do bad things happen to good people? The quick answer may be, "Well, it's all about karma." And when we give this response, again it feels as if we can make some kind of sense out of the suffering. After the tidal wave in Southeast Asia, there were a significant number of postings on Buddhist websites struggling to explain why all those people were killed. There were several very respectable writers proclaiming that it was the karma of the people who died that they would be swept away in a tidal wave. They were fishing for a living, and there is a Buddhist precept about not killing, so somehow their deaths made sense in the big picture. Other websites explained that it must have been something they did in a past life. The concept of karma can easily become an explanation that will make us feel safe because it appears that somewhere there is a reason—it's our karma—and, if we believe this, then, once again, we can find some kind of order in the world.

So, for this good man I told you about—David—was it his karma that brought on the attack? Did he do something bad by being so helpful? Should he have known better than to be kind to that particular young boy? If David didn't do anything bad, and if the Buddha said, "With our thoughts we make the world," then how do we make sense of David's injuries, his suffering? With his thoughts, did he make the world that involved an attack upon him? How do we understand this teaching without assigning blame when difficulty happens? It's wonderful to think we create our reality when things go well; it's not so easy when life is painful.

Remember, again, that it's natural to want our lives to make sense. It's instinctive to reach out for answers, and it's very easy in looking for responsibility to have that search segue into blame, within about three seconds! We blame others; we blame ourselves; we use the idea of karma or God's will to justify this urge to blame. We want to blame someone because it hurts, because we want the world to make sense, and because, otherwise, it can sometimes feel unbearable.

I read a very touching question in "Annie's Mailbox" recently. The writer said to Annie: "I just lost my son to alcoholism. He was 55 years old and for five years had been progressively drinking himself to death. We were totally unaware. His multitude of friends and business associates knew he had an alcohol problem, but didn't realize the gravity of the situation and didn't think to notify me, his father.

"My son was divorced, had no children and lived alone. I've since been told that I couldn't have done much unless he was willing to admit he was an alcoholic and wanted to quit. I'm a well-educated person, but didn't know the true symptoms of alcoholism. My son is dead, gone from my life because I didn't know how alcoholics act and think. *My friends tell me not to blame myself. But who else is there?*" (italics mine).[34]

Life can feel so painful sometimes that we feel we've *got* to have an answer, any answer at all. Whose fault is it? Mine? Yours? God's? Who is to blame? How can we make sense out of this really terrible pain? If the Buddha taught that we are what we think, with our thoughts we create the world, then we can easily believe we must have somehow "created" what happened to us. This is a natural human response to suffering.

I'd like to suggest that there is another way to understand the Buddha's words—a way in which we can pull apart, I hope, this very common merging of thoughts that says, if we are what we think, then we must be creating our own reality. First, let's look briefly at the concept of karma. It seems to me that we can understand the idea of karma to mean simply that this is a lawful universe. "Lawful" in the sense that what happens comes out of all the events that went before. In other words, when one thing happens, then the next thing happens: cause leads to effect. But there are two significant caveats to this description. A very important one is that we never know all the factors involved in any particular event. I find that the longer I live, the more I don't know much about why anything happens. Life is so complicated and so complex and when we say that one thing obviously caused something else, well… I'm not so sure anymore. I don't know what all the causes are for the events of life. So, given this complexity, the second part of the understanding of karma, as I see it, is that it is not an idea formulated to fix blame or responsibility in one place. When we experience pain or fear or anger our human minds usually want to find someone to be responsible, someone to blame. But I don't think karma is about blame. It's actually quite neutral. Karma is simply descriptive of the radically complex nature of life—it recognizes all the elements that go into every action, every event, every reaction.

What then is the meaning of this Buddhist teaching, if not that we create our own reality? I would suggest that the words "with our thoughts we make the world" are a statement about how our thinking directly affects what we perceive in life, and that our perceptions, in turn, affect what we experience to be happening. In other words, I think it's a statement about process. And the process of thought is where we have a choice. I don't think we always have a choice about the content of our lives. In fact, probably most of the time we have very little choice. The content of events is the external, more-or-less-verifiable happenings in the world. But the process of our minds is the way we experience our lives. In other words, there may be hatred around us—this is the content. But, if we train our minds to hate, if we cultivate a mind of hating—this is the process. And there's a very big difference between these two things.

Here is what Martin Luther King said in a sermon he gave at the Dexter Avenue Baptist Church in Montgomery, Alabama, on Christmas in 1957 (Keep in mind that he wrote this while he was in jail for committing nonviolent civil disobedience during the Montgomery bus boycott.): "To our most bitter opponents we say, 'We shall match your capacity to inflict suffering by our capacity to endure suffering. We shall meet your physical force with soul force. Do to us what you will, and we shall continue to love you. We cannot in all good conscience obey your unjust laws because noncooperation with evil is as much a moral obligation as is cooperation with good. Throw us in jail and we shall still love you. Bomb our homes and threaten our children, and we shall still love you. Send your hooded perpetrators of violence into our community at the midnight hour and beat us and leave us half dead, and we shall still love you. But be ye assured that we will wear you down by our capacity to suffer. One day we shall win freedom but not only for ourselves. We shall so appeal to your heart and conscience that we shall win you in the process and our victory will be a double victory.'"[35]

He said, "We shall win you in the process." The content he is speaking about is racial hatred and bigotry, yet the process of his mind was to choose not to hate in return. With his thoughts he made his world. And, through his process of mind, we know he did make the world a different place than it had been before he lived.

Here's what I'm saying: we do not often have a choice about what life brings—about the content of events. But we do have a choice about how we direct our minds. And that choice determines in good part what we experience in our lives. Our choice is about the process of our own minds.

So, let me finish my original story. This good man, David, was attacked, and it was a very traumatic experience for him. He immediately did everything he could to work with it. He made a full report and it was confirmed that what he saw that night was indeed what had happened. He testified at the trial. He felt frightened, and he admitted this to himself. He felt angry, and he admitted that. He wanted to blame himself, and he worked with this, and it has taken a very long time. Here's what he said to me several years later: "I wondered if the message was that I should not be trusting, that I should not be kind, but I am not willing to think that way. I am not willing to live in that place in my mind." His recovery has been slow, and often grim. He's worked and worked to pull apart the threads of blame and worry and anger and fear. He's had to try enormously hard to understand that he is not responsible for the content of that experience. But he has been and continues to be willing to work with training his mind in the process of how he understands it.

"We are training our minds," the Buddha taught. "With our thoughts we make the world." In awareness, we have a choice about how we will direct our thoughts in response to life. If we do not pay attention, as David Foster Wallace says, we will be operating on our "default settings," which "[hum] along quite nicely on the fuel of fear and contempt and frustration and craving and the worship of self."[36] Wallace goes on to say: "The really important kind of freedom involves attention, and awareness, and discipline…awareness of what is so real and essential, so hidden in plain sight all around us, that we have to keep reminding ourselves over and over:

"'This is water.'

"'This is water.'"[37]

My friends, this is our water. This is what we get to notice. These are our minds. For the most part, we cannot choose what happens to us. We cannot choose the content of external events. But we *can* choose how we will direct our minds. We *can* choose the process of our own minds. We are what we think. The way we experience life arises with our thoughts. With our thoughts, we make our world.

# 9

# Open to the Outcome

We've been looking at the Buddha's teaching that our minds shape our experiences of life. Now, this is a very direct statement about the nature of existence. It gets our attention. It can be a bit intimidating; but I find also that it's incredibly inspiring. It suggests that we have the wonderful possibility of affecting the process of our minds. We can work on cultivating awareness. We can truly learn to quiet our minds and open our hearts. We can feel so much better. In fact, the metaphor used is that happiness will follow us like our shadows, unshakeable. Isn't that wonderful? And, yet, it's amazing to me how this very teaching can also lead to our own suffering. This is what I'd like to consider a bit more: how we sometimes take this teaching and, without meaning to, use it against ourselves.

It happens like this. As we begin to understand and to recognize that we are indeed what we think, that our thoughts generate our experience of the world, then the very next thing that can arise for us is, "Well, then, I just need to have the right thoughts! If I only think good thoughts, if I always have wise thoughts, or compassionate thoughts, or thoughts filled with loving-kindness and courage and inspiration, then everything will be fine. After all, the Buddha said, 'Happiness will follow us as our shadow, unshakeable.' So when I have only pure thoughts, then I will only feel the happiness that arises with a wise heart, and with an aware mind."

In the early years of Zen practice in this country, in the sixties and seventies, we had a slightly different way of casting it. We thought, "I must reach this experience of supreme enlightenment, and then I will be happy. Then everything will be permanently wonderful, because I will have broken through to this ultimate and unchanging understanding. Then my life will be perfect." Whether we couch our desire to end suffering as sudden enlightenment or as a permanently kind mind, it still can come down to this: when we do *not* experience the desired state of mind—including having this state of mind last forever—it can feel as if we must be failing.

A psychiatrist and Zen teacher in New York City, Barry Magid, calls this phenomenon, "spiritual anorexia." He writes: "practice [can] become[s] a high-minded way of purging ourselves of aspects of ourselves that we hate." For example, "We may have had the ideal that practice will make us compassionate, and so we end up trying to do away with our self-centeredness or even do away with our desires—but in doing so, we set up one part of the self in opposition to another part."[38] This is an accurate description, don't you think? We can easily try to get rid of what we don't like within ourselves, and this creates a struggle in our own being, in our own mind. We set up one part of our self in opposition to another part. If we believe that only good thoughts are acceptable, then we will and must wall off whole parts of ourselves that are "unacceptable."

I experienced this in a very vivid way the first time I received a cancer diagnosis. Someone put a series of tapes in my hands with teachings from a man named Bernie Siegel. At that time, he was a popular speaker about working with cancer, and his theme was that he had known people whom he called ECaPs—Exceptional Cancer Patients. These were the patients in his practice who always thought positively, who absolutely directed their lives toward healing, toward getting rid of their cancer. They never gave way to negative thinking. Siegel asserted that the results in overcoming cancer were far better for ECaPs because they had a positive attitude all the time. He counseled those of us who were cancer patients to undertake this practice, to be an ECaP—an Exceptional Cancer Patient—and think only positive thoughts.

As I listened to the tapes, a small fear began to grow in me: "Maybe I can't be an ECaP!" I couldn't always have positive thoughts. Sometimes I was frightened. Sometimes I felt resistance. Surely, this would prevent me from healing my cancer. I found myself feeling more frightened, not less. What if I couldn't have the right frame of mind to be a survivor? Finally, I confess, I threw the tapes away. I realized that, for me, the only way I could be with this cancer was to tell the truth to myself about what I was feeling, and the truth was that I didn't have only positive thoughts. I didn't have continually pure thoughts. I didn't always have healthy thoughts. I was often terrified. This was the truth. I had to tell myself the truth. It was frightening to say this at a time when the power of positive thinking—at that point, we called it New Age thinking—was being strongly urged upon us all.

This teaching—we are what we think—can become a terrible double-edged sword if we don't pay close attention to what we are saying to ourselves. If we choke off the terrified thoughts, if we wall off the angry thoughts, the fearful thoughts, the discouraged thoughts, we are engaged in an act of mental and emotional purging. If we only find certain thoughts and experiences acceptable—those that are good or kind or compassionate, for example—we will begin to experience, as with physical anorexia, a profound weakening in our lives. If we constantly reject our experience, reject what is true for us, we can begin to die inside. In the early years of Zen in this country, this teaching of spiritual anorexia was often expressed this way: whatever your difficulties are, this is your practice. And, of course, this is true in one sense. But we understood it to mean that if we were feeling discomfort, then we needed to learn to think differently. It was *our* problem. We needed an attitude adjustment, or in other words, "Just get over it."

Spiritual practices, unfortunately, can be a strong path to self-rejection. In our very longing to do better as human beings, and to live with more happiness and with less suffering, we can do great harm to ourselves. We want to do well, perhaps to not "sin," in the Christian sense, or we might couch it as being kind or compassionate or patient, and when we try and try and still discover that we cannot once-and-for-all be that way, it's very easy to punish ourselves.

Now this may sound melodramatic, so I want to talk about it in very everyday terms. Here's what I experience in my life: I am so much happier than I ever used to be, thanks to this practice. I notice things more quickly. I choose much more frequently to not go off on a long riff of mind chatter. But, the fact is, it's not always that way. I do my best, but sometimes I get discouraged. Sometimes I worry about where our country is going, about what we are doing as humans on this planet. Sometimes I notice thoughts of resistance, of dislike. And then I notice that I don't want to feel that feeling. I don't want to feel this resistance to my life. I don't want to feel impatience, or all the other uncomfortable feelings that arise. I can observe the thought arising in me, "Here's this discomfort, and I don't want to feel it. I'm happy to be aware, but I don't want to be aware of *this*."

It's the not-wanting-to-feel-*this* feeling that is so important to look at, because, right in that moment, we reject not just the experiences we are having—the particular thoughts or feelings that are coming up—but we can easily reject our own minds. We can set up a pattern, a habit, of rejecting ourselves. "I shouldn't have *these* thoughts. They should be gone by now. I've done this practice for so long—I should be doing better." Discouragement, self-blame, dissatisfaction—these are often subtle markers of self-rejection, what Barry Magid calls "spiritual anorexia."

What is the alternative to this mental rejection? How else can we respond to our lives? There's an indigenous teaching attributed to the Maori tribe in New Zealand that talks about four steps we can practice in living our lives well. The fourth step is expressed as being willing to be "open to the outcome." Being open to the outcome in our lives means being open not just to what we want, but to what we get: this is the outcome—whatever happens. I think it's a wonderful teaching, and I've been increasingly realizing how demanding it is. The outcome is not just some final grand and glorious time in the future when, yes, we can be equanimous and enlightened; the outcome is every event, each small happening, each tiny outcome, in every single day—nothing special—imagine being open to this too!

A poem by William Stafford has this line: "Are you waiting for time to show you some better thoughts?"[39] Good question—are we waiting for time to show us some better thoughts than the ones we are having right now? Are we waiting for our minds to think in a different way, or for our hearts to feel more equanimous or more forgiving than we actually feel? We're waiting. And we keep waiting. We can say, "Yes, I plan to accept my life—definitely I plan to be open to the outcome—but couldn't I just have slightly different circumstances to accept? Couldn't I feel a little bit better first, and then I will gladly be open to it all?"

 I have a friend whom I'll call Hannah. I spoke with her recently and learned that her life is much the same as usual, meaning that, yes, she is waiting for life to show her some better thoughts, different from the ones she usually has. Hannah is in her sixties and is still waiting to meet the love of her life. I asked if she'd met any interesting men recently. She replied, "Not yet. I haven't met anyone yet because I'm waiting to feel better than I do now, and then I know I will find him." Hannah has a Christian practice, and she said, "I realize I'm waiting, of course, but I'm waiting for grace to enter my life"—not Grace, the person, but the grace of God—"and then I know this new life will be possible. I'm waiting to feel differently about myself, and then things will change." Hannah is indeed waiting for time to bring her some better thoughts, and this is so very easy to do. We may all find ourselves waiting for time to show us some better thoughts. We can notice this hope, when we don't want to feel *this,* and we don't want to feel *that,* and not *this* and, also, not *this.* Just, please, something different from what's actually happening!

If we consider being really open to the outcome, we're talking about something we could call acceptance. And I think acceptance is very difficult. We have to start with accepting ourselves, and this definitely includes accepting the ordinariness of our minds and of our lives. Do you ever think to yourself, "But it's all so very ordinary? Couldn't my life be just a little more interesting than it is?" Here's what I'm concluding: we're not going to get it all together—this life—and we're not going to get over it either. Probably, for most of us, grace is not going to descend upon our minds in the near future. It's likely that we're not going to always feel peaceful and never get discouraged or be disappointed. As a great Christian mystic said, sometimes we will feel "cut off from God." Or we might say that we will not be able to always find a quiet mind and an open heart. Not all the time.

This is the demanding daily practice of real acceptance, and it's not a passive act. Are we waiting for time to show us some better thoughts? If so, we had better wait sitting down. Here's my point: these are the only thoughts we've got. And these are the only minds we've got, and the only hearts. I notice how often I would just like to feel a little bit differently than I do. I would like not to feel a particular feeling—discouragement or fatigue or confusion. I would like a slightly different outcome than the one I'm experiencing. This is the place of practice: not coming to another mind, but coming to this mind, our mind.

I am convinced that equanimity is my choice, that no one else can give it to me, and that, if I don't choose it, I *will* have an unquiet mind. It's just that I have so much trouble remembering that I have to keep choosing it, moment by moment. I'd prefer to make a permanent choice—one solid, blissful experience. I want to get it over with, once and for all. No one ever told me that with all these big important turning points, I'd have to keep turning. But it's true. We have to keep choosing, every single day. Open to the outcome is a moment-by-moment practice. We seldom get great big outcomes to which we can be open; we get little ones, day in and day out.

I'm learning that acceptance is like meditation, and it's like brushing our teeth. We just have to keep doing it, over and over. Is there a time when we can stop brushing our teeth? Maybe a few days before death—but we don't know when that will be. Otherwise, we have to keep brushing. We have to keep meditating. We have to keep accepting every day. Do you know what else it's like? It's like loving someone. We have to keep stepping into it. We have to keep trying again and again. Many of us have a wedding ceremony, and it feels like such a big and glorious commitment, but, then, day by day, we have to keep remembering to love, to choose again and to choose again, moment by moment. We use words like *acceptance* and *forgiveness*. We use words like *love*.

I come back often to Henri Nouwen's saying that "forgiveness is the name of love practiced among people who love poorly." So, too, is acceptance. The hard truth is that all of us love poorly, and accept poorly. As Nouwen says, "We need to forgive and be forgiven every day, every hour—unceasingly."[40] We need to keep accepting our lives, over and over. Otherwise, it's very easy to begin practicing spiritual anorexia, to reject just a little bit here and a little bit there, and then a little bit more. The name of love, the practice of acceptance, is what we do with our own minds, with the discouragement and the anger and the fatigue and the wanting—the wanting, the endless longing for things to be different than they are. This is the practice of acceptance, of being open to the outcome. We're never going to just get over our minds. Rather, I think what we have is the possibility of choosing to get *into* our minds. We have to swallow it all, over and over, minute by minute, swallowing this and swallowing that—this very mind, the only one we've got.

# 10
# When the Heart Closes Down

I was talking with a very fine person recently, a woman who has dedicated her whole life to helping others. She told me how important it feels to her to make the choice, over and over, to keep trying to be of benefit in the world. "It's so clear when we look closely," she said, "that compassion is what's needed in this world." Then she continued, "Knowing this, I find myself wondering, asking myself, why is it so hard for me to remember this, to act on this understanding? Why do I keep forgetting?" It's a good question.

Here's someone else, reflecting on the same topic: this is from an NPR interview with a federal court judge who was discussing his many years of service on the bench.[41] The interviewer asked what he thought might be common mistakes that judges make. The judge replied that two issues seemed important to him. One was that it's difficult to be patient. He spoke about this for a bit, but then he went on at greater length about the second challenge. He said it's especially difficult for a judge to maintain compassion for the person in front of him or her, the one being sentenced. He said that judges know the penalty of federal prison is harsh, and it's difficult to face the person being sent off to prison and remain compassionate. Isn't that interesting? It's difficult to maintain compassion for the person we must judge. He was suggesting that being the one to pass the sentence could have the emotional side-effect of closing the heart. This person has made his life one of service to others, and, like my friend, he says it's difficult to keep the heart open.

I remember hearing someone say once that it's quite painful to forgive someone whom *we* have harmed—not the other way around, not the person who has injured *us*—but the person *we* have wounded. I've noticed a version of this: when I feel as if I've compromised myself somehow, my heart feels especially closed to the person who simply stimulated my own feelings of inadequacy. I find it harder to like someone, to remain compassionate, when I connect this person with my own lack of awareness or compassion.

This is a really important issue to consider. Don't we all know that compassion is the essential healing medicine for this suffering world? Yes, we know this; we really do. Then why is it so difficult to act from this knowledge, and to live in the light of this awareness? Why is this so particularly challenging? My friend asks this question, the judge reflects on this issue—why does the heart close down?

I was listening to a talk by Karen Armstrong, a scholar who has written extensively about the Abrahamic religions.[42] She was a nun herself as a young woman until she left the convent in her mid-twenties. After her departure, she went through a period of great disillusionment with the Catholic Church, but gradually found herself coming back to religion as a force in the world, and one that she could relate to, through the scholarly work of studying and writing. In this speech, she talked about what she considers the core teaching of all three of the Abrahamic religions—Judaism, Islam and Christianity. She said that, until quite recently—about the seventeenth century—none of these religions were demanding or expecting belief in the way that we think of it now. Apparently, the original word *belief* carried the meaning "to love" or "to hold dear." She said that religious practice was thought to be about living this life, in the sense of *behaving* differently. Religion meant the effort to act out of love. The early doctrines in all three of these religions were really a summons to *action*.

She went on to say that the central action called for is compassion—to "feel with" another—and that within these three religious systems, this was how people learned to come into the presence of God. This was the act of faith required of the practitioner: one entered through the doorway of compassion. When I grew up in the Baptist church we called it The Golden Rule, but whatever we want to name this state of heart and mind, it's truly the core of these spiritual traditions—to feel with, to cultivate, compassion. Armstrong emphasized that these earlier religious practices depended upon a willingness to *act upon* the sense of "feeling with," of compassion. This meant to do unto others what we would want to receive ourselves, or sometimes it's been stated in the negative: do not do unto others what you would not wish to receive yourself.

Of course, we also know that the injunction to act with compassion is absolutely central to what the Buddha taught. Certainly, the Dalai Lama speaks about this regularly. For example, he writes in his book, *Ethics for a New Millennium*: "Compassion is one of the principal things that make our life meaningful. It is the source of all lasting happiness and joy....we can reject everything else: religion, ideology, all received wisdom. But we cannot escape the necessity of love and compassion."[43] These are very important words—we cannot escape the necessity of love and compassion.

This woman I spoke of earlier said, "It's clear when we look closely that compassion is what's needed in this world." Then she paused and shook her head before saying, "But why is it so hard to remember this? Why is it so difficult to act upon this understanding?" It's an important question. Why is it so difficult to live out our beliefs? Why is it so hard "to love and to hold dear?" We have the best of intentions, and then, in an instant, the heart can close down, we can lose our compas-

*A Light in the Mind*

sion. Why do we practice for years and years and then find ourselves doing exactly the same thoughtless or careless action that we did twenty years ago? Why do we continue to create suffering in our own minds when we really know better?

I must tell you, I don't have one single response that can address the depth of these questions. Of course, we could come up with a lot of different speculative, theoretical or explanatory answers, but when we emphasize the question "Why?" we often stay in the realm of intellect, of mind, of theory, of explanation. In my experience, knowing the available answers and running through them all can become a bit like checking off items on a list. I can theorize about my lists, ponder all the possible ways to improve my life, and speculate about reasons for this or that, but it doesn't change the shock I feel when I find myself doing the same old unskillful action.

Here's another way to put this: focusing on the question "Why?" doesn't seem to change the issue of "That." That it happens again. That I—and all of us at times—shut down. Reasons don't touch the pain of my closed heart when it's happening. At the moment it's happening, it just is. So, let's ask instead, how does it *feel*? What is this experience where the best part of our self wants so much to care, to love and to hold dear, and then we can't seem to follow through? What is this experience of failure to feel adequately with the world? What is it to withdraw from our human connections, to isolate, to fall asleep in the world and in our lives?

My experience of this failure of compassion, this failure to feel with the world, is that it arrives completely unbidden and happens in an instant. It almost always takes me by surprise. Actually, most of the time I can step back and see the situation and recognize my responses—maybe fear, or outrage, or shame, or anger—but, nevertheless, each time my heart closes it's a shock. And it can happen especially quickly when interacting with the world. My mind can be pretty steady when nothing special is happening, when I'm all by myself. But interacting with others is almost always, by definition, rather unexpected and new, and perhaps frequently a bit startling. I find that in just one moment, one unexpected, unprepared-for moment, I can lose my focus, forget, and fail to maintain compassion with the world. It's really easy for this to happen in daily life.

When I think about how it feels to lose awareness, to fall away from compassion, it feels to me like falling asleep and then waking up to the rupture in instant pain. This is a really important experience for us to pay attention to: this caring and loving and holding dear, and then the unexpected failure of this most basic human connection.

And here's what I see—this failure is actually a central core of our humanity. I'd like to think that simple compassion is the core of our humanity, but I suspect that the rupture in compassion is *equally* our core. This moment when we blink our eyes, this moment when we fall asleep, seems to me an unavoidable part of being human.

Here's a key point: our failure to love is exactly where we who undertake a spiritual practice can work with training ourselves. Oddly, this may be exactly what we are seeking, because it is the place, the event, the blink, the sleep that makes waking up most possible. It's so painful to feel this rupture in compassion over and over within ourselves, yet we are truly finding exactly what we are looking for. We are locating this one person and this one place where we can most fully and deeply learn to love.

We know the word *compassion* means "to feel with," but the challenge is to feel with *ourselves* at the moment we enter into this rupture of our own compassion. What a practice this is! We're told the Buddha taught that we could look the whole world over, and we would never find another person more worthy of our forgiveness, of our acceptance, of our compassion than ourselves. So, right in the heart of the break, in the collapse of our own compassion, exactly here is where we can find an important place for forgiveness, for acceptance. We can look the whole world over, and never find someone else more worthy of our compassion than ourselves.

Karen Armstrong talked about the necessity of compassion within the Abrahamic religious practices as being compassion for the other, and, in some ways, I suspect that compassion for someone else may be a little bit easier to cultivate than compassion for ourselves. We can usually either create a little more distance from the other person, or we can come in closer, and in this mental movement we may often find a way to feel compassion for another's suffering. But compassion for this own self—to feel with our own selves while we also recognize that our very failures are generating exactly the pain we don't want to feel? This is really difficult!

And it can seem confusing emotionally, to practice being kind to ourselves in the moments when we cannot be kind to others. This is especially true given the injunctions that many of us heard, perhaps, as we were growing up, not to be self-centered, not to be selfish. Maybe young people don't hear that quite so much anymore, but I remember phrases like, "Don't be conceited! Don't be so full of yourself!" Do you remember hearing those comments? It might seem that what I am suggesting here is a contradiction. Aren't we trying to learn to love others and not be so self-centered?

Actually, I suspect it's more of a paradox than a contradiction. I believe we do want to reduce suffering in the world. We are trying hard or we wouldn't be practicing in this tradition. And we do care for others. If we were truly self-centered we might well choose a more pleasurable route to acceptance, such as possessions, power or luxury. But the paradox is this: kindness to our self—this self that we so carefully construct, this self that is, according to *The Heart Sutra*, empty of solidity—kindness to this self that can often hate others and reject others and feel no compassion at all seems to be the most direct route to loving others. I find that if I want truly to feel with others and to cultivate compassion, I have to start by feeling it for my own flawed and failing self first. When I can practice being with my own failure with clearer eyes, somehow it seems to crack my heart open, at least for a time...at least for a time. I suspect this may be as good as it gets.

Now I want to be very clear. I'm not talking about making excuses for what we do. And, on the other hand, I'm not talking about feeling guilty for how we act. This is a very tough-minded stance, actually. It demands the willingness to look deeply and honestly into our own hearts and minds, to own every inadequate and failed thought and action that we can, and *to do this without self-pity and also without self-guilt.* I'm not suggesting indulgence, the passive thought of, "Oh well, whatever!" And I'm not suggesting condemnation, "I'm such a lousy human being!" Instead, it's no excuses and no blame. This is a very active acceptance of our lives. Just this. This is what it is. And here it is. Look again. And look again. We own it all. All of it. No excuses and no blame.

So, here's what I notice: there's a deep source of compassion right in the center of this practice. We keep training ourselves to pay attention, to look again, to notice our feelings and thoughts. We bring our attention in, very close. We practice observing the first flickering awareness of comfortable and uncomfortable, of positive and negative—these most primitive first feelings. As we pay more and more attention to our own minds—to the beginnings of our reactions to life and to the cascades of feelings and thoughts and actions that flow forth—when we practice doing this, we cannot help noticing our failures of compassion. They are right in front of us.

I find it becomes clearer after years of effort that we are not going to become different persons from the ones we are. We're not going to change into someone else, becoming that other person we think we might rather be. The only thing left is to *accept* our lives, these very lives, these limited bodies, these minds, these hearts, these constructed selves. And here's the paradox I'm speaking about: right here—in this acceptance—is the freedom. Right here is the forgetting of self. Here in the knowing that this is *all* there is and that this is *what* there is—this failed and inadequate being—just here is the compassion for each of us. We are going to be ourselves. We are going to be exactly who we are.

I'm suggesting that the teaching is really this: we must commit ourselves to compassion—as the Dalai Lama urges us, as the Buddha urges us, as all great religious traditions urge us—we must commit ourselves to training our hearts and minds in awareness, and, as we do this, we come to the point of really knowing, nevertheless, that no matter how hard we try, we are going to fall asleep sometimes. We are going to fail. This is what there is. And this is all there is. There is no other place of perfection that we will reach. Please, if there is anything I can say that will relieve your suffering, it is this: *give up the pursuit of perfection!* Wherever we notice that we feel we are failing, right there, is the key to entering the Kingdom of Heaven, as the Christian teachings might say, or, entering into Nirvana, as the Buddhist Sutras suggest—not wanting life to be different than it is. Not judging ourselves. Not judging others. We accept our lives directly out of our own failures. Let's not wait until we get everything all together.

So I encourage you to look closely, to be willing to be with your pain, because it's exactly here that we stand up again. Exactly here—when, for a time, we fail in our most essential effort to be compassionate—here is where we must make the effort, one more time. And it is exactly here, in this noticing, that we once again have the opportunity to recover our compassion. This is the heart of our practice, our actual home. Welcome home!

# 11

# Have I
# Done Enough?

Kobun Chino Otogawa Roshi, my teacher, spoke about this practice we undertake in Buddhism when he said, "The more you sense the rareness and value of your own life, the more you realize that how you use it, how you manifest it, is all your responsibility. We face such a big task, so naturally we sit down for a while." It *is* a big task, manifesting our lives, so I agree. Naturally, we sit down for a while. And then there's this as well: facing such a big task, naturally, also, at some point, we must stand up again. Sometimes we stand up unexpectedly in response to events; sometimes we stand up with joy. Sometimes we stand up more slowly, perhaps with resistance. But the pivotal point is that we keep trying. We just keep trying. I would suggest that what matters most is our intention. We intend to keep making our best effort. We intend to stand up again, in our lives.

Sometimes it's difficult to know what's skillful to do when we stand up. Sometimes our efforts are not directed in the best or most helpful ways, but I think we want to do better or we wouldn't be undertaking this practice. I would ask you to think about the painful thoughts that occur to you. Aren't those thoughts somehow interwoven with wanting to do better? "We face such a big task, so naturally we sit down for a while." And, naturally, also, we stand up again. Mostly, we just keep trying. This is our intention, and intention matters.

Here's a very touching story from Pico Iyer's book *The Open Road*. He writes in the first chapter about visiting the younger brother of the Dalai Lama, whose name is Ngari Rinpoche. This brother has been an assistant to the Dalai Lama for years. He's trained with him, and works with him. He's turned his whole life over to the same enterprise as the Dalai Lama in support of Buddhism and Tibet. In this chapter, Pico Iyer writes about visiting with Ngari Rinpoche one evening at his home in Dharamsala. There's a huge storm and all the power is out, but, nevertheless, they go, Pico and his partner Hiroko, to share dinner with Ngari Rinpoche.

He says: "We retire after dinner to the living room for tea and suddenly, with his characteristic directness, our host turns to me in the near dark.

"'Do you think I've done anything for Tibet?'

"'Of course,' I say, stumbling a little, because taken aback. 'You've been an intermediary between Tibetans and the Western world.'

"'Oh,' Rinpoche says, 'you're saying I'm just a Westerner.'

"'No.' Less trained than he at ritual debating, I fumble for a second. 'But you can take information to His Holiness that he wouldn't hear otherwise.'

"'He has other people who can do that for him. Take my word for it.'

"I shuffle uneasily in my chair, hoping he'll change direction.

"'You're being polite,' he goes on (and again I think of his brother's impatience with mere formality). 'Mine is the serious question. Do you think I've done anything to make Tibetan lives any better?'

"'You have, by knowing the world outside Tibet.'

"He laughs dismissively, as if I've hit an easy serve ten feet over the line. We go on talking for a while and then Hiroko and I make our way back to our little room in the guesthouse up the hill. As we get there, I recall how I have heard almost exactly the same sentence fourteen years before, from the Dalai Lama, the day after his Nobel Peace Prize had been announced. 'I really wonder if my efforts are enough,' he had said, at the very moment when he was being most feted by the world. All we can do, he had told me, is try, even though it sometimes seems to be in vain."[44]

"I really wonder if my efforts are enough," the Dalai Lama says. Receiving the Nobel Peace Prize, he raises the question, "But have I done enough?" You and I wonder about our lives, and he wonders, also, how can we do just a little bit more? How can we relieve pain—our own and others? How can we face our minds and this life? Have we done enough? These questions arise so easily and so naturally. They express our intention to make our best effort, and—here's an interesting thing—in the very questions themselves, we can see how we are feeding and generating the mind of dissatisfaction. If only I could do one more thing—this is the subtext—if I could achieve one more object or reach one more goal, or if only I could believe that I'm doing enough. Even the best people question whether they're doing enough, and, in a sense, it seems to highlight our perpetual minds of dissatisfaction—these very human minds.

A. H. Almaas, the founder of Ridhwan teachings, has suggested that this desire to do better—at its best, we could say it is the wish to be of service—has perhaps the unintended consequence of leading us out of the present state of our lives into what he sees as a dual rejection. In wanting to do better, we create a sense of a deficient self, as we are, and the possibility of a perfect self, which we would like to be. We reject the deficient, the not-good-enough self; we desire the ideal self of accomplishment. And, in both cases, we are stepping out of the present into an alternative, created idea in our minds. Harvey Aronson summarizes Almaas's comments in this way: "Rejection and hoping are inextricably linked with creating a sense of self."[45] Here we are, back again, to this question of the self, our creation of the self as it is expressed in our longing for fulfillment. The Dalai Lama asks if his efforts are enough, and we ask this, too, about life. Is it enough? Is this life enough as it is? I take comfort from knowing that the Dalai Lama asks this question also. It seems natural to me that we ask this. It seems very human.

So, here's the Buddha with a teaching that goes right into the heart of this question: he says that the self is not solid but, rather, is more accurately a patched-together process. Let's look at this for a few moments. Our self—this self that seems solid and continuous, and more like a thing or an object, not like an event or a process—this self is actually fragments of experience pasted together in a way that creates a *feeling* of solidity. It's similar to the way individual pictures, with only a slight change from one to the next, are run very closely together and all of a sudden we experience them as a movie. One event occurs, then another and another, in a continuous series of happenings, and it seems as if there's a real "thing" happening. Our experience of our lives is as compelling as a very good movie. We're sitting in the theater and these huge bright images move smoothly in front of us, and it's so incredibly easy to be pulled into the seeming reality in front of us. We think that this *must* be our life.

When I was a young girl my father had one of those enormous movie cameras people used back then and a big projector. He loved making and playing those movies—all the clicking parts, the spinning wheels—and he made lots of home movies about our family. I especially remember my brother, my mother and I walking down the steps from our house on Sunday morning, dressed in our new Easter finery on our way to church. I recall that we had to practice walking up and down a lot, to get it just right. Then my father would play it over and over for us to watch. We found it fascinating, and we'd watch the same movie week after week. But the machinery was a bit clumsy and things would go wrong. I remember that the film used to break a lot. We'd be watching our movie, when, suddenly, we'd hear a shudder and a click, and the film would break. In place of us walking down the steps, there would be a bright blank light on the screen. Or, at the end of the spool of film, there would be a few numbers on the screen, and, again, the bright blank light. So here was what looked like the real thing happening, and then, all of a sudden, a gap, a break would open up. It was quite often literally a break in the film itself. When we watch our lives carefully, sometimes we experience these same gaps, these breaks in the events of our lives. We can see the flickering between the images, and, for a moment or two, we understand that these are separate events and tiny little breaks keep occurring between them.

I've spoken about experiencing, about noticing, the rupture in compassion that can happen for us. Even our most dearly held intentions sometimes break apart. "Things fall apart, the center cannot hold," William Butler Yeats wrote.[46] One of you spoke to me about feeling almost as if you have a dual self—one that cares so much and the other that feels as if it breaks apart, as if the self splinters. This can be frightening sometimes.

To continue this film metaphor, we might say that we instinctively tend to paste together these discontinuous pictures. Perhaps you've experienced what I have, that we can hear what we expect to hear, or see what we expect to see, even when our eyes and ears literally tell us something quite different. In other words, it's easy to complete our internal stories, even with no external confirmation. And this is definitely true with the self. We complete the discontinuous self. Everything goes by so quickly that it looks real. And we learn to fill in the blanks.

So, why does this matter anyway? What difference does it make whether we are solid, stable, real things, or whether we are more discontinuous events? Here's why it may be important: if we are solid and real, then we should actually be able to mould and sculpt and polish the self we want. We should be able to succeed at making this solid self, this wonderful creation, be exactly what we want, because the real stuff is there out of which we should be able to carve ourselves. When we watch very closely, however, we see that this solid self keeps shifting. It's slippery, and it slides around. The Buddha was teaching that this belief that we are solid and perfectible, and that life can be manipulated and can be something that we can manage or control—this belief itself is what causes our suffering. We are told that he said to his disciples, "Look closely and tell me. Can you find a self that is solid and permanent and wonderful and happy?" and his disciples looked, and they said, "No. No, Master, we can't find that." But don't we want life to be that way, nevertheless? I certainly do. And right here is our suffering. Looking at it very directly, if we want what is impossible, we will only want endlessly. This is a magnificent setup for suffering.

Another way to look at it is that it's actually a huge relief to recognize that we can't manage this life. It's a relief, because it means we aren't particular failures when we can't get life to "work" for us. Even if we can't find what we want, or be who we want to be—even if we feel these scary feelings of fear and longing, or discover that we have an angry or grief-stricken outlook on life—even so, what we can see is that these qualities we think of as weaknesses or inadequacies are really just the nature of the human condition.

Let me ask you: what do you wish you could change in your life? What do you wish you could do differently? *Exactly this* is your entry key into the house of the human family. What do you feel guilty about? What do you hide from others? What parts of yourself are you ashamed of? This is who we all are. And this is not personal to you. This is the really good news about our fractured lives. When our lives are painful, it's not our own particular failure. We are simply human, and we are all in this together. We fail, over and over again, and this is the way life is. This is the heart. This is really the secret deep inside life itself. This flickering, this breaking apart, this failure, this rupture—this is the way it is. It's not our personal and private mistake.

Here is an important passage from Henri Nouwen: "Forgiveness is the name of love practiced among people who love poorly. The hard truth is that all of us love poorly. We need to forgive and be forgiven every day, every hour, unceasingly. This is the great work of love among the fellowship of the weak that is the human family."[47] The hard truth is that we all belong to this human family. We need to forgive and be forgiven, and we need to forgive ourselves, over and over and over. This is the experience of being human. As far as I can tell, being alive is just this: effort, intention, inevitable failure, and, finally, the need for forgiveness.

Now, I'd like to put these thoughts in the context of meditation practice, because it's very important that we understand what it is that we're doing here, as much as we can. Here at Everyday Dharma we work with two different streams of meditation practice, two different forms that come out of the traditional Buddhist schools: Mindfulness or Vipassana meditation from the Theravadin tradition, and Stillness Abiding, a version of *Shikantaza* from the world of Soto Zen Buddhism.[48] One of my favorite Vipassana teachers in this country is Joseph Goldstein. I've heard him teach several times, and each time, he has uttered a very important sentence: "Everything rests on the tip of motivation." In other words, our willingness, our intention, is the place to which we must return, over and over, in order to do this practice. And he's right. Everything rests on the tip of motivation. Until we can bring our intention, our motivation, our willingness into our practice, I think it's really impossible to cultivate the kind of stable effort that will enable us to be aware of our experience. It's in establishing a continuing awareness that we begin to notice the nature of this being that we call "ourselves"—this collection of energy, this gathering of events spliced together, again and again. In other words, we will never notice the gaps and ruptures unless we keep watching all the time. The Buddha said, "Pay attention. What do you experience when you watch your mind?" Everything rests on the tip of motivation—this is central to Mindfulness practice. It's essential to awareness. Another way to put this would be to say that we need to care over and over. We need to return to trying endlessly. This is the path to mindful awareness in our lives. This is the practice of Vipassana.

And then we have *Shikantaza*, our practice at Everyday Dharma that we call Stillness Abiding. Do you remember Kobun's translation of the mantra at the end of the Heart Sutra? He said the last few words meant: "Falling apart, falling apart, everything is falling apart. Everything is always falling apart. Nothing to do." With those last words, "Nothing to do," we come directly to Stillness Abiding, the practice of not doing anything. Nothing. No thing to do. It's a practice in presence and in stillness and in not doing any one particular thing.

So, if Mindfulness is a practice that depends upon trying, on motivation and the willingness to keep going, then Stillness Abiding is our most direct training in giving up the wanting of any particular outcome. Maybe we're giving up hope for a better future in which everything will at last be fixed and wonderful. Or maybe we're giving up a longing for a better past, a wish that things could have been different for us than they were—so that we could feel more accepting of our lives. With Stillness Abiding we are literally practicing the act of *being*—of not going anywhere else with our minds and our experience.

And this is the paradox of practice. Paradox—from the Greek word *paradoxon*—which means "beyond what is thought." We are holding two opposing possibilities in our selves, simultaneously. One is that we must make our best effort; we must keep trying. And the second is that, in this very same moment, we must also give up wishing for things to be different than they are, give up believing that somehow we can fix life or make it be better than it is. This is definitely beyond what we usually think!

How can we do this? How can we find the energy and the willingness to keep trying, while not wanting and longing for things to be different than they are, especially as a result of our effort? It's a daunting task, a challenging task, and a subtle state of mind. And, actually, in the moment of failure, in the moment of losing our direction, when our effort collapses and we recognize it—this is the place we really feel what it is to belong to the human family. We experience not only the gaps in the self, but also the unending gap between what our lives actually are and what we would hope for them to be. Finally we get to face the impossibility of holding things together.

*A Light in the Mind*

The Dalai Lama says, "I really wonder if my efforts are enough." It seems to me that here, too—not just for us, but even for the Dalai Lama—the only answer is the answer of compassion. For all of us. Forgiveness, as Nouwen said, is the practice of love in the fellowship of the human family. We get to practice forgiving these weak, cobbled-together selves. We get to practice accepting this patched-together process that we call "I" and "others" and "you," all of us, each of us—a patched-together process, a cobbled-together self, a collection of frequent failures—those of us who love poorly, all of us who love poorly. This is the fellowship of the weak which is the human family.

So, this is what we do—we stand up again. And we stand up again, together. We stand up again over and over, and I think we can do it best together. I haven't found a better way, and, believe me, I've looked. Here. Take my hand, and I'll take yours, and let's stand up again…together. This is the best we can do, and it is truly good enough.

# 12

# A Light
# in the
# Mind

We've been talking at Everyday Dharma about the question raised by the Dalai Lama after he received the Nobel Peace Prize. Even as he was being feted by the whole world, he found himself wondering if his efforts truly had been enough. When we slow down, when we stop and pay attention, it's possible to feel the wish arise that somehow we might do more, or do better. Perhaps it seems we should be doing something else, something other than this life we find ourselves experiencing. Are we getting it right? Most of us want to feel accomplished, to seem worthy in our own eyes and in the eyes of others. And it's easy to long for life to have transcendent meaning always. Couldn't we just be certain that what we're doing is enough, or is the right thing? These feelings are often just a quiet moment or two away from our consciousness.

We could say that, in its most general form, it's a desire for our lives to be extraordinary somehow. So, here at our Zen Center, we've been considering what it might mean for each of us truly to accept and to allow ourselves to be something else—to be ordinary. What if we're not really special at all? What if we're quite ordinary? For some of us, this can bring a sense of deep relief, because there's no need to strive so hard, to feel always dissatisfied and fearful of criticism; it's actually all right just to be ourselves. For others, being ordinary can feel truly disappointing; the words that come to mind are *boring, dull, uninteresting*. We look around at others in the world, and it can seem that, here and there, some people truly are different—larger than life, we might say. So why can't we also be one of these very extraordinary people?

I remember the many years I felt a deep longing to be special, to be extraordinary. Growing up in post-World War II America, I, along with many of my generation who came of age in the sixties and seventies, wanted to be anything but ordinary. Looking back on my life, I'm sure that this was involved in my desire to practice Zen Buddhism. It looked so special—there were mysterious ways of talking and sitting, and the monks all had striking black robes to wear. The retreats were heroic, with very little sleep, cold feet and brutal conditions. Surely if we undertook all these special practices, we could be extraordinary, even luminous perhaps? Couldn't we then reach an ideal, transcendent state of mind?

When I first met my teacher, Kobun Chino Otogawa Roshi, it seemed that all my wishes to find transcendence came together in his very presence. He appeared to be absolutely extraordinary. This slight Japanese man was, for us, the perfect expression of mystery. He moved silently, except for his rustling robes; he chanted in ancient languages; he gazed at us with large, luminous eyes; and it felt to me as if, merely by looking at me, he could penetrate into my very heart and mind. He was incredibly exotic; he wore white *tabi* socks and carried a teaching stick. He'd grown up in a Zen temple family in Japan, and we knew he'd begun to meditate when he was less than six years old. I think I believed that simply being in his presence would somehow help me transform my life into something extraordinary. I suspect most of us who were his students felt this way in the beginning.

Fortunately for us, Kobun was an amazingly kind person. He didn't take advantage of our adoration; he was very accepting of us at our little *zendo* in Santa Cruz. We were a motley gathering of hippies, graduate students, short-order cooks and carpenters, and, nevertheless, he was willing to be completely present with us in our ordinary lives. He gave us the great gift of living his life in our midst. We who were his students spent time with him when he was glorious and inspirational, and we felt inspired simply by being around him. In looking back on this time, I think that we felt touched by his reflected glory.

But there was this also: because he was willing to stay connected with us, slowly, gradually, by paying close attention, we could also begin to see not just the glory in his presence, but also sometimes the sadness in his eyes. Occasionally, he seemed isolated, even in the midst of many people. We began to notice that his life didn't always work out so perfectly; he too sometimes seemed to fall apart. He couldn't hold everything in his complicated world together all the time. Apparently, life for him was also what we might call "ordinary." It could be painful and difficult for him, too.

I experienced Kobun as being incredibly present and accepting of us, an amazingly kind man. I also realized gradually over the years, that he was, just like all of us, a very ordinary, flawed human being. He made mistakes. He suffered. His life story looked quite different from ours in the details—more glamorous to us perhaps—but it was the same in effect. We are, each of us, ordinary human beings. We all carry the weight of our family and our personal stories. We all make mistakes, and we all suffer. This seems to be built in to being alive.

I think this was his greatest gift to me, actually. Finally, I understood that there was no other, more perfect life to reach, beyond this ordinary embodied experience. If Kobun couldn't do it—if he couldn't attain a blissed-out state of permanent wisdom and serenity that would protect him from pain in his life—then it was very unlikely that I would find such a place myself! When I recognized this, I saw that there was nothing else to wait for: this life is it. Right here and right now. This is what there

*A Light in the Mind*

is. Rain on the roof. Newspaper soaked and muddy. Unopened mail, unfinished lives. This is what we have—birth and death and everything that lies between. The nature of this life is that it is flawed, it is modest, it is often unsatisfactory. And, also, this life is of enormous value. Nothing is special. And yet everything is unique. This is what we have in these very ordinary, embodied lives. I learned this, in being with Kobun.

Knowing that what we have—*all* we have—are these ordinary lives, I feel now how important it is to not take what we have for granted. Let's not think that everything will always be the way it is when life feels good. No one person, no particular thing, no place of practice will always be waiting for us. When Kobun died, I was incredibly shocked. I had thought that he would always be there for me. I must confess that when I learned of his death, my first thought was horror that he had died; and my second thought was, "But what about me?" I realized, as I sat with his death, that I had taken him very much for granted. Having learned this painfully with Kobun, I want to say, let's try not to do that. Don't think that everything will always be the way it is now, that we can always count on life being the way we want it to be. This is the only time we have, and this is the only life we have, so let's not take anything for granted.

Now, say we really don't want to wait to live our lives, and we truly have the intention not to take things for granted, then the question is, how exactly can we do this? If we look at our ordinary lives, what might this mean? Certainly I have asked this question for years. How do we do this thing of being alive? What are we doing? In fact, I would say that, as a group of students around Kobun, we asked that question of him more frequently than we did any other. We phrased it in many different ways, but it came down to something like this: "Kobun, why do we sit? Why do we do this practice? Why do we meditate?" Over and over, for thirty years or more, we returned to this most basic question.

In looking back through the many years that I knew him, I can see that Kobun's answers grew and deepened over time, just as his life changed and transformed. When he arrived here in America, he was a single, young Japanese man who had grown up in a traditional Asian temple world and had undertaken Buddhist training and studies. His spoken English seemed to be largely scholarly, and his conceptual framework was fairly abstract. I must confess that I found him very difficult to understand in the early years. Here is a portion of a talk he gave that illustrates this time period. As usual, we were asking, "Why do we do this? Why do we sit?" He replied, "The stage of purity go endlessly and so-called 'Nirvana' comes very end of it. Nirvana is literally 'death,' perfect death is what Nirvana is, and we accomplish it before this body reach to end—still functioning remain we reach to that end of purity." I really didn't understand what he was saying! I had trouble retaining the words. I noticed instead that, for me, the real importance of what Kobun taught was in the way he lived with us; still, I longed to "understand" what he was saying. When, occasionally, he would utter words that I could actually absorb, I felt how precious they were. I suspect it was that way for most of us who were his students. We hoarded the few words we understood.

In retrospect, I realize that, over the years of his teaching, his English became much clearer, and his expressions were increasingly less abstract and more grounded in his experience. Here is the way he answered this same question, "Why do we sit?" in the middle years of his teaching: "The main subject of *Denko-e* [a particular retreat period] is how to become a transmitter of actual light. Life light. Practice takes place to shape your whole ability to reflect the light coming through you and to generate, to re-generate your system so the light increases its power." Now, that was much clearer for me than his earlier statement! It was an image that I could really understand and remember.

There are two aspects to this description that I'd like to mention. One is the emphasis on light—this was a very important, recurring image for Kobun. He used the word frequently in his dharma talks, and also in conferring names. *Ko* is the Japanese sound for "light," and he named his two practice places *Hokoji* and *Jikoji*. My dharma name also has the word *Ko* in it, as well—*Eiko Joshin*. The possibility of light was very important to Kobun. Transforming and enhancing light was his goal.

The second aspect is the feeling of power and strength he conveyed when he spoke about "generating, re-generating [our] system so the light increases its power." He spoke about this in the prime years of his teaching; he was strong and pursuing a life of doing it all. He was committed to having a family and, at the same time, being an available and connected teacher. He traveled from place to place; he took care of his children; and he ministered to his large *sangha*. He believed—we all probably believed at that time—that it was possible to do everything we set out to do. In fact, Kobun seemed actively to embody this principle for many of us. When he said, in effect, practice is about taking the light that shines into us and making the light even stronger, it felt as if he were actually casting a bright light of inspiration directly upon us, his students. We each drew comfort and clarity from him; he truly seemed to lighten the world around him.

We're told that the Buddha, in his final teaching words, used a similar image. Sometimes it's translated as, "Be a refuge unto yourself." But often his words are rendered in this way, "Be a light unto yourself. Make of yourself a light." Maybe we can understand it as this: make a greater brightness in the world—find your own way.

I've mentioned that when we asked Kobun how to do something, how to do a ceremony for example, he would reply, "You figure it out. We're making it all up as we go along." And, if we really understand that, then of course we have no choice but to find our own way in this life. We must find the light within ourselves. We must be our own light. Kobun liked to say that our effort to find our way, to create a greater brightness in the world, was a natural impulse. In this same teaching about being a transmitter of light, he said, "We face such a big task, so naturally we sit down for a while." We were constantly asking him, "Kobun, why do we sit? Why do we do this practice?" His answer was that, facing such a big task as living our lives, naturally, we sit down for a while.

So, here is this practice that we do, this deceptively simple activity: we sit down; we slow down; we reduce the stimulation in our lives; and, for this period of time, we give up distraction and entertainment. We simply sit still, making the effort, over and over, to just be here, in this present moment. As you know, this is amazingly difficult. I think that's why, for so many years, we all kept asking Kobun again and again, "Why do we do this?" We might have been saying, "Why on earth should we do this, at all?" It's certainly the hardest thing I've ever done, finding the willingness, over and over, to sit down again, to be present in my life, just as it is. Actually, we could also say, just as we are.

And when we just sit down, this is what happens: we experience the pain that we've been suppressing, the grief we haven't had time for, the anger we've hidden away, the fear that constantly shadows us. We discover that our minds do their absolute best to escape being here; and we also realize that we—whoever "we" are—are not in charge at all. Over time, we begin to notice also how much we can actually love others and perhaps finally ourselves. We begin to see that we can turn directly into our pain; we can feel it fully and, even so, we can still survive. When we walk toward our fear we discover that we are no longer controlled by our fear. The fact is that however much we are able to be present—exactly that much is what we are able to bear. Even the death of a most beloved teacher is finally bearable. This was exactly what I found with Kobun after his death. Sitting down—practicing—gave me a way to hold all the feelings so they didn't destroy me, and I didn't have to run away. With practice, we can begin to see our lives more clearly, and to live these lives with greater freedom because we are learning to be present. This is truly a revolutionary secret.

In "The Buddha's Last Instruction," Mary Oliver describes the final teaching from the Buddha: "'Make of yourself a light,' / said the Buddha, / before he died…. / An old man, he lay down / between two sala trees, / and he might have said anything, / knowing it was his final hour."[49] The teaching of a lifetime comes down to this one suggestion: "Make of yourself a light. Be a light unto yourself." Find your own way, we might say. Mary Oliver concludes her poem by speaking in her own voice: "clearly I'm not needed, / yet I feel myself turning / into something of inexplicable value."[50] In fact, although clearly none of us are needed, amazingly enough, as we quiet our minds and open our hearts, we can truly feel ourselves turning into something of inexplicable value. Kobun pointed us, his students, in this direction. He said that practice is about receiving the light that comes into us, and increasing the power of this light. "Make of yourself a light," the Buddha said. "Be a light unto yourself." Be of value.

In the 1980s, Kobun moved away from northern California, from us, his students in the Bay Area, but he would sometimes come back, perhaps once a year, for a *sesshin*, a retreat. Most of us carefully kept our calendars clear for his return, and carved out the time to go to see him. I certainly did that. I found that I might have the opportunity to talk with him perhaps for one hour a year during that time when he was gone. That was all. I treasured that one precious hour so much; I would remember for months afterward what he had said to me.

Then, in the late 1990s, something amazing happened. He actually moved back to this area, and lived quietly for several years right here in Santa Cruz, up in the small community of Bonny Doon. He settled with his new wife and second family into a traditional-style Japanese farmhouse, only about five minutes from my home. It was quite startling and wonderful to have him so close once again.

After he had been here for several months, I asked if it would be all right to get the old-timers together to sit with him occasionally; he quietly nodded his assent. There were about ten of us who had sat with him for many years, and we began to meet once a month on a Sunday afternoon at my house, just to have the opportunity to sit together again as a *sangha*, and to be with Kobun. I look back now and I realize how unique this time was. To use Kobun's own words, it was "a rare and precious opportunity." We did this as a group for maybe a year and a half, perhaps two years, until Kobun and his family moved to Colorado.

Death comes unexpectedly, doesn't it? At our last meeting with Kobun—we didn't know it was our last meeting at the time—someone once again asked that old familiar question, "Kobun, why do we sit? Why do we do this?" Now, you've already heard two of his answers—the first one abstract and perhaps difficult to understand, and the second one inspiring and dynamic. At this final meeting, he gave us a third answer, the last one I heard from him. It seems to me that this response expresses his mature reflections, gathered over a lifetime of living. What he said was concrete and easy to understand; and it was, to my ears, humble and deeply touching. I don't know if anyone else wrote down his words, but I did, as soon as I could find pencil and paper. I'd like to share his precious final response to our perennial question, "Why do we do this practice?"

"We sit," Kobun began slowly, "to make life meaningful. The significance of our life is not experienced in striving to create some perfect thing." He looked down at his hands as he spoke. He was quiet for a long time. Then he continued, "We must simply start with accepting ourselves. Sitting brings us back to actually who and where we are." Again he waited, as he perhaps reflected upon his own life. "This can be very painful. Self-acceptance is the hardest thing to do." Once again, he paused, so long at this point that I wondered if perhaps he had finished. But finally he continued, "If we can't accept ourselves, we are living in ignorance, this darkest night. We may still be awake, but we don't know where we are. We cannot see. The mind has no light." He stopped and looked around at us in our small circle. He moved from face to face with his eyes, seeing deeply into each one of us, his long-time, oldest students. Finally, he nodded slightly, and concluded, "Practice is this candle in our very darkest room."

Here it was, Kobun's conclusion to a lifetime of practice and teaching:

"We sit to make life meaningful. The significance of our life is not experienced in striving to create some perfect thing. We must simply start with accepting ourselves. Sitting brings us back to actually who and where we are. This can be very painful. Self-acceptance is the hardest thing to do. If we can't accept ourselves, we are living in ignorance, this darkest night. We may still be awake, but we don't know where we are. We cannot see. The mind has no light. Practice is this candle in our very darkest room."

It's so simple, isn't it? We sit to make life meaningful. Practice brings a modest light into our minds. Yes, a simple teaching. And, for me, the most profound one. I had listened to Kobun speak about Buddhist practice for thirty years, and, as I reflected at that last meeting upon his teachings, I finally saw and felt something of the sweep of his life. It seemed to me that his mind had transformed in a phenomenal way. He had moved from the traditional abstract Zen way of speaking in both content and presentation, all the way, we could say, to the practice of the tender heart. It was an amazing journey for him to take. It was a profound evolution. When I considered how far he had traveled in his experience, beginning in the very traditional Japan before World War II, I was incredibly inspired. And the fact that he would talk about it—this very private man—made it an enormous gift to us, his students.

Let's look closely at his words, this final teaching. He begins, "We sit to make life meaningful." We practice to understand our lives, we could say, to find a meaning or a purpose in our lives. Actually, we sit so that life *has* meaning. We sit in order to love our lives, to treasure this transient life. And then he goes on to say something so important: "The significance of our life is not experienced in striving to create some perfect thing." I looked at Kobun's quiet face, the sadness that sometimes was visible in his eyes, and I knew that the significance of Kobun's life was clearly not in what he had created, not in some perfect thing, but was simply in who he was. He certainly didn't create a perfect life. In many ways, it was a life of chaos. But that wasn't what mattered. We loved him for who he was when he was with us. And this is what mattered after he died. Not some perfect thing he'd created, but simply his willingness to be with us, to love us unconditionally.

He continued by saying, "We must start with accepting ourselves," and I knew that Kobun spoke from his own experience. There were profound ways in which he suffered in his life, and I considered it one of his greatest teachings that this man we loved so much, who held us with such great kindness, also had to struggle to accept himself. It was difficult even to see that this was what was happening. It was difficult to believe it. And, yet, it was true.

He went on to say, "Sitting brings us back to actually who and where we are." In other words, when we sit down, when we sit still, we find out what's really going on. We experience what's true in our lives. Then he continued, "This can be very painful. Self-acceptance is the hardest thing to do." He was talking about the minute-by-minute willingness to be who and where we are, without turning away, without blotting out our consciousness, without judgment and without despair. This is really challenging.

Then he came back to the image of light, and you'll notice that this time it was not as a great transformer; rather, it was as one small candle. "If we cannot accept ourselves, we are living in ignorance, this darkest night. We may still be awake, but we don't know where we are. We cannot see. The mind has no light." If we can't accept ourselves, he was saying, we are living in darkness, a great darkness of the mind and of the heart. It is a big task, learning to accept ourselves, so, naturally, we sit down for a while. And, then, his last sentence came back to our old, perennial question: why do we sit? Why do we make this effort to sit down, to quiet the mind and observe what is happening? Because, "Practice," he said—this meditation, this effort, this awareness and stillness—"is this candle in our very darkest room." Practice creates the smallest light in our darkness. This effort at awareness and stillness is our one single candle in the darkness of our minds and hearts. You know, when we have all the electric lights turned on, a candle doesn't seem like very much light. But when the power goes out, have you noticed how much light a single candle brings? This is what he finally came to in the course of his life: practice brings us one small candle in the darkness of our minds and hearts.

Here's what I would suggest: we don't have to be huge floodlights. Let us just be small and ordinary candles. "Make of yourself a light," the Buddha said. "Be a light unto yourself." We sit down in the darkness of our lives, and our practice is this one small candle that helps bring us light and clarity and understanding. We sit and sit, knowing that we're not needed—knowing how ordinary we finally are—and yet, gradually, ever so gradually, we find ourselves turning into something of inexplicable value. Ordinary, yes. And priceless too, each of us.

Kobun was my teacher of inexplicable value. With his life, he lit one candle in the great darkness in which we all sometimes found ourselves. I miss him so much. Once again we light our one ordinary candle, each of us, in our darkest rooms; every day, this day, we discover a small light within ourselves when we naturally sit down for a while. "Make of yourself a light," the Buddha said. "Be a light unto yourself." Let us each care for our one small candle in the darkness of our minds. This is the light of practice, the light of awareness and of stillness—one small light of inexplicable value.

Practice creates a light in the mind.

*We sit to make life meaningful.*

*The significance of our life is not experienced*
*  in striving to create some perfect thing.*

*We must simply start with accepting ourselves.*

*Sitting brings us back to actually who and where we are.*

*This can be very painful.*

*Self-acceptance is the hardest thing to do.*

*If we can't accept ourselves, we are living in ignorance, this darkest night.*

*We may still be awake, but we don't know where we are. We cannot see.*

*The mind has no light.*

*Practice is this candle in our very darkest room.*

**Kobun Chino Otogawa Roshi**

(1938–2002)

*Concluding Teaching from Kobun Chino Otogawa Roshi*

# Acknowledgments

At Everyday Dharma Zen Center, we frequently speak about the great gift of the *sangha*, the community of practitioners who support our lives. I feel enormous gratitude for the many people who make up this *sangha* for me. You were all instrumental in creating this book.

I am deeply grateful to my teacher, Kobun Chino Otogawa Roshi, who pointed the way toward practice. His gentle presence was a warm light for those of us who were his students. And my children and their families continually teach me about being alive; I love you so much, Nathan and Seth, Julie and Grant.

This book would not have been written without the steadfast effort of the members of the Dedicated Practitioners group at Everyday Dharma. They enable me to return, over and over, to this experience of paying attention in my life. The people who come to sit at Felsentor in Switzerland each year are equally an inspiration. We who are teachers can't speak if there is no one to listen.

My dharma brother, Vanja Palmers, is endlessly generous—a special thanks for permission to use the picture of Kobun from the website *Kobun-sama.org*. My good friends Guenter Illner and Richard Zenki at Felsentor always provide essential support for my teaching there. Many other friends here in the United States offer their kindnesses regularly. And my husband, Alan Richards, makes everything possible—writing, teaching, living this life.

Finally, the publication staff worked again with amazing skill and equal generosity: Kay Clark, Becky Luening, Suzanne Schrag and Cliff Warner.

This book only exists because of all of you. I am deeply grateful.

Carolyn Atkinson
Santa Cruz, California
February 2010

# References

Chapter 1

1  Matsuo Basho haiku, in *The Essential Haiku: Versions of Basho, Buson, and Issa*, ed. and transl. Robert Hass. Hopewell, NJ: Ecco Press, 1995, p. 11.

2  Gerard Manley Hopkins, "God's Grandeur," in *Poems*. London: Humphrey Milford, 1918. Online version: http://www.bartleby.com/122/7.html.

Chapter 3

3  For example, Kimberly Lankford, "Weird Insurance," *Kiplinger's Personal Finance Magazine*, October, 1998. http://findarticles.com/p/articles/mi_m1318/is_n10_v52/ai_21136401/

4  "Publican Insures Against Ghosts," BBC News, 5 April, 2002. www.bbc.co.uk/2/hi/uk_news/england/1913960.stm

5  Ibid.

6  Lankford, op. cit.

7  Helen Keller, *The Open Door*. NY: Doubleday & Co., 1957, p. 17.

Chapter 4

8  Rabbi Joseph Gelberman, quoted in *How to Forgive When You Don't Know How*, by Jacqui Bishop and Mary Grunte. Barrytown, NY: Station Hill Press, 1993, pp. 9-10.

Chapter 5

9  Margaret S. Mahler, Fred Pine and Annie Bergman, *The Psychological Birth of the Human Infant: Symbiosis and Individuation*. NY: Basic Books, 2000.

10 David Schnarch, *Passionate Marriage: Love, Sex, and Intimacy in Emotionally Committed Relationships*. NY: W.W. Norton, 1997, p. 56.

11 William Safire, "The Bush Comeback," *New York Times*, February 7, 2000. http://www.nytimes.com/2000/02/07/opinion/essay-the-bush-comeback.html

12 Melody Beattie, *Codependent No More: How to Stop Controlling Others and Start Caring for Yourself*. NY: Hazeldon, 1992.

13 Terry Burnham and Jay Phelan, *Mean Genes: From Sex to Money to Food: Taming our Primal Instincts*. NY: Penguin, 2000.

14 Ibid., p. 113.

15 Ibid., pp. 5-6.

16 Ibid., p. 252.

17 Harvey B. Aronson, *Buddhist Practice on Western Ground: Reconciling Eastern Ideals and Western Psychology*. Boston & London: Shambala, 2004.

18 Ibid., pp. 1-2.

19 Lao Tsu, *Tao Te Ching: A New Translation*, transl. Gia-Fu Feng and Jane English. NY: Vintage Books, 1972, Verse Number 9.

Chapter 6

20 Aronson, op. cit., p.65

21 Carolyn Atkinson, *Quiet Mind, Open Heart: A Practice Period in Meditation*. Santa Cruz, CA: Everyday Dharma Zen Center, 2008, pp. 95-96.

22 Pico Iyer, *The Open Road: The Global Journey of the Fourteenth Dalai Lama*. NY: Knopf, 2008

23 Pico Iyer, *Video Night in Kathmandu: And Other Reports from the Not-So-Far East*. NY: Vintage, 1989.

Chapter 7

24 David Foster Wallace, *This Is Water: Some Thoughts, Delivered on a Significant Occasion, About Living a Compassionate Life*. NY: Little & Brown, 2009.

25 Ibid., p. 8.

26 http://www.viewonbuddhism.org/resources/buddhist_quotes.html

27 Thomas Cleary, transl. *Dhammapada: The Sayings of the Buddha*. NY: Bantam Books, 1995.

28 Wallace, op. cit., pp. 98-101.

29 Thich Nhat Hanh, "Our True Home," in *Best Buddhist Writing 2007*, ed. Melvin McLeod. Boston: Shambhala, 2008, pp. 82-88.

30 Ibid., p. 88.

31 Atul Gawande, *Complications: A Surgeon's Notes on an Imperfect Science*. NY: Picador, 2002.

32 Ibid., p. 20.

33 Wallace, op. cit., pp. 128-132.

Chapter 8

34 "Ask Annie," *Santa Cruz Sentinel*, Tuesday, April 21, 2009, p. B4.

35 Dr. Martin Luther King, Jr., "Loving Your Enemies," sermon delivered at the Dexter Avenue Baptist Church, Montgomery, Alabama, Christmas Day, 1957. http://salsa.net/peace/conv/8weekconv4-2.html

36 Wallace, op. cit., p. 115.

37 Ibid., pp. 120, 131-33.

Chapter 9

38 Barry Magid, *Ending the Pursuit of Happiness: A Zen Guide*. Boston: Wisdom Publications, 2008, pp. 8-9.

39 William Stafford, "You Reading This, Be Ready," in *The Way It Is: New and Selected Poems*. St. Paul, MN: Graywolf Press, 1998, p. 45.

40 Henri Nouwen, "The Only Necessary Thing: Living a Prayerful Life," in *Selected Writings of Henri J. M. Nouwen*, ed. Wendy Wilson Greer. NY: Crossroad Publishing Company, 1999, p. 153.

Chapter 10

41 http://www.vpr.net/news_detail/84137/.

42 http://www.ted.com/talks/karen_armstrong_makes_her_ted_prize_wish_the_charter_for_compassion.html.

43 His Holiness the Dalai Lama, *Ethics for the New Millennium*. NY: Riverhead Books, 1999, p. 234.

Chapter 11

44 Iyer, *The Open Road*, op. cit., pp. 29-30.

45 Aronson, op. cit., p. 76.

46 William Butler Yeats, "The Second Coming," in *The Collected Works of W. B. Yeats: Volume I, The Poems*, 2d ed., ed. Richard J Finneran. NY: Simon & Schuster, 1997, p. 189. (First published in *Michael Robarts and the Dancer*, 1921.)

47 Nouwen, op. cit., p. 153.

48 Atkinson, op. cit.

Chapter 12

49 Mary Oliver, "The Buddha's Last Instruction," in *New and Selected Poems*. Boston: Beacon Press, 1992, pp. 68-69.

50 Ibid.